TENNESSEE TRIVIA

REVISED EDITION

TENNESSEE TRIVIA

**COMPILED BY
ERNIE & JILL COUCH**

REVISED EDITION

Rutledge Hill Press
Nashville, Tennessee

Published by Rutledge Hill Press, 513 Third Avenue South, Nashville, Tennessee 37210

Typography by Bailey Typography, Nashville, Tennessee

Library of Congress Cataloging-in-Publication Data
Couch, Ernie, 1949–
    Tennessee trivia / compiled by Ernie & Jill Couch.—Rev. ed.
        p. cm.
    ISBN 1-55853-109-2
    1. Tennessee—Miscellanea. 2. Questions and answers.
I. Couch, Jill, 1948– . II. Title.
    F436.5.C68 1991   91-8994
    976.8'0076—dc20   CIP

Printed in the United States of America
1 2 3 4 5 6—96 95 94 93 92 91

PREFACE

When *Tennessee Trivia* was originally compiled, it became evident that many volumes could be written about this fascinating state. Tennessee has a colorful and compelling history based on a richly diversified land and people. Now the revised edition of *Tennessee Trivia* captures even more interesting facts about this exciting heritage.

    Tennessee Trivia is designed to be informative, educational, and entertaining. Most of all we hope that you will be motivated to learn even more about the great state of Tennessee.

Ernie & Jill Couch

To our son Jason
and
the great people of Tennessee

TABLE OF CONTENTS

GEOGRAPHY

C H A P T E R O N E

Q. What is the greatest distance between the northern and southern borders of Tennessee?

A. 115 miles.

Q. What was the name of the utopian community founded in 1880 in Scott County by author Thomas Hughes for young English gentlemen?

A. Rugby.

Q. The lowest point of elevation in Tennessee is found in what county?

A. Shelby County, 182 feet (55 meters) above sea level.

Q. What large military reservation is situated near Clarksville and extends into Kentucky?

A. Fort Campbell.

Q. What is the present name of Burrville, named in 1801 in honor of Aaron Burr?

A. Clinton.

Q. In what county was Tennessee's first Masonic lodge?

A. Williamson.

Q. What was the name of the self-governing independent community established in 1772 by John Sevier and James Robertson in what was to become eastern Tennessee?

A. The Watauga Association.

Q. Charles D. Little of Chattanooga, who organized the Good Grape Company and the Seminole Flavor Company, experimented with a new taste until he finally developed what new soft drink?

A. Double Cola.

Q. What city is recognized as Tennessee's oldest town?

A. Jonesborough.

Q. Where is a United States Naval Air Station located in the state?

A. Millington.

Q. What community is noted for pencil manufacturing?

A. Shelbyville.

Q. Near what present-day community was Davy Crockett born?

A. Limestone.

Q. What present-day tourist area was noted for producing bar iron in the early 1800s?

A. Pigeon Forge.

Q. How many acres encompass the Land Between the Lakes?

A. 170,000.

Q. What is the present name of the college situated in Jefferson City and formerly called the Mossy Creek Missionary Baptist Seminary?

A. Carson-Newman College.

Q. Where did James K. Polk practice law from 1841 to 1844?

A. Lewisburg.

Q. What was the first city-owned park for blacks in the United States?

A. Hadley Park, Nashville.

Q. In which two counties is Chickasaw State Park located?

A. Hardeman and Chester.

Q. Where was the first Methodist Episcopal Church erected on Tennessee soil?

A. Acuff Chapel in Sullivan County.

Q. The Natchez Trace State Park is found in what county?

A. Henderson County.

Q. Who was the woman known as Mrs. Methuselah who was born in Germany in 1688 and died in the community of Lawrence in Maury County in 1835?

A. Aunt Betsy Trantham, at the age of 147.

Q. What is the highest road gap in the state?

A. Newfound Gap, elevation 5,048 feet.

Q. In what county was longtime standing speaker of the House of Representatives Sam Rayburn born?

A. Roane County.

Q. Norris is the location of what museum?

A. The Museum of Appalachia.

Q. What town is named for a famous Polish general of the Revolutionary war?

A. Pulaski.

Q. What university is located in Clarksville?

A. Austin Peay State University.

Q. What town is named after the Aluminum Company of America because of the massive aluminum reduction plants in that area?

A. Alcoa.

———◆———

Q. Where does Tennessee rank in size among all the states?

A. Thirty-fourth.

———◆———

Q. What name did Hernando de Soto give the Mississippi River upon viewing it for the first time on May 21, 1541, from the lower Chickasaw near present-day Memphis?

A. River of the Holy Ghost.

———◆———

Q. What was the name of the principal town of the Cherokee Nation, situated in present-day Monroe County, during the seventeenth century?

A. Great Talequah.

———◆———

Q. In what county did John and Rebecca Crockett, parents of Davy Crockett, establish and operate the Crockett Tavern?

A. Hamblen County.

———◆———

Q. Which two black religious publishing houses are located in Nashville?

A. The National Baptist publishing house and the African Methodist Episcopal Church publishing house.

———◆———

Q. The nation's oldest and largest military park is found in what city?

A. Chattanooga, Chickamauga and Chattanooga National Military Park.

Q. What was the first name of Nashville?

A. Fort Nashborough.

Q. In what county would you find Minnie Pearl's Grinder's Switch?

A. Hickman County.

Q. What is the greatest distance between the eastern and western borders of the state?

A. 480 miles.

Q. Who from Dandridge organized the Atlanta National Bank and became its first president?

A. Alfred Austell.

Q. What was the whirlpool and rapids that created navigational difficulties where Suck Creek enters the Tennessee River called?

A. The Suck.

Q. What street was made famous by composer W. C. Handy?

A. Beale Street.

Q. Carter Caves State Natural Area is located near what community?

A. Sherwood.

Q. What is the only town in the United States with elevated second-floor sidewalks in the downtown business area?

A. Morristown.

Q. How long is the Tennessee River's main navigational channel?

A. 650 miles.

Q. Where was Chet Atkins born?
A. Luttrell.

Q. What amount did the Transylvania Company pay the Cherokees in 1775 for all the lands between the Kentucky and Cumberland Rivers?

A. 2,000 pounds sterling and goods worth 8,000 pounds.

Q. Where is the only state-operated ferry across the Tennessee River situated?

A. Clifton.

Q. For what reason was Martin Luther King, Jr. in Memphis at the time of his assassination?

A. To support the strike of city sanitation workers.

Q. Lueveney K. Riley was the first woman street cleaner superintendent of what community?

A. Hornbeak.

Q. What is the name of the town founded in 1869 in Grundy County by one hundred Swiss families?

A. Gruetli.

Q. Candy's Creek Cherokee Indian Mission was situated in which county?

A. Bradley County.

Q. What is the oldest registered distillery in the United States?

A. Jack Daniels Distillery, 1886, Lynchburg.

Q. The state of Tennessee boasts approximately how many incorporated cities?

A. About 300.

Q. In what year was the first bridge in Nashville built to cross the Cumberland River?

A. 1822.

Q. Where was guitarist Lester Flatt born?

A. Foothills of Overton County.

Q. What was the occupation of Elihu Burritt, through whose effort Burritt College was established in 1848 to allow youth in Van Buren County an opportunity for an education that was denied him?

A. Blacksmith.

Q. What city is known as the "Queen City of the Cumberland"?

A. Clarksville.

———◆———

Q. The twenty-five-foot national monument to Meriwether Lewis, co-commander of the Lewis & Clark Expedition, was placed above his grave in what county?

A. Lewis County, named for Meriwether Lewis.

———◆———

Q. What is the Tennessee state motto?

A. Agriculture and Commerce.

———◆———

Q. What county has the distinction of using the oldest courthouse built in the state?

A. Dickson County, 1833.

———◆———

Q. What is the name of the highway running from Nashville to Natchez, Mississippi?

A. The Natchez Trace.

———◆———

Q. What city of 3,600 residents is annually visited by more than four million people?

A. Gatlinburg.

Q. What was the name originally given to the hill upon which the State Capitol now stands?

A. Cedar Knob.

Q. What was the address of the law office of Andrew Jackson in Nashville?

A. 333 Union Street.

◆

Q. What is the height of Fall Creek Falls, the highest waterfall east of the Rocky Mountains?

A. 256 feet.

◆

Q. When Judge John Overton purchased 5,000 acres from the Chickasaw Indians, which later became the city of Memphis, how much did he pay for it?

A. $500.

◆

Q. Where in Tennessee is the "world's largest fish fry" held?

A. Paris.

◆

Q. The illustrious military personage, politician and diplomat, Isaac Shelby, has counties in how many states named in his honor, including Shelby County in Tennessee?

A. Nine states.

◆

Q. The Tennessee–Tombigbee Waterway connected what two locations?

A. The Pickwick Lock and Dam (Tennessee) and Demopolis, Alabama.

◆

Q. What state park received its name from an eight-foot-tall sandstone rock, preserved in Monterey, that served as a boundary marker between two Indian tribes?

A. Standing Stone State Park.

Q. What renowned summer resort was called the "queen of the hill country in Tennessee"?

A. Beersheba Springs.

———◆———

Q. The ancient stone fortification and moat of unknown origin called the Old Stone Fort is found where?

A. Manchester.

———◆———

Q. Where was Roy Acuff born?

A. Maynardsville.

———◆———

Q. James Sevier, the first governor of Arkansas, was born in which Tennessee county?

A. Greene County.

———◆———

Q. What Franklin County landmark, which housed a restaurant that employed mentally handicapped adults, was rebuilt after it was destroyed by fire in 1990?

A. 100 Oaks Castle.

———◆———

Q. On February 24, 1861, what Tennessee county brought before the then Confederate State of Alabama a petition to annex it?

A. Franklin County.

———◆———

Q. What was the name of a Presbyterian colony from South Carolina which located in Maury County in 1807?

A. Zion.

Q. What was the name of the former county seat of Shelby County in which Aaron Burr was imprisoned for a short time?

A. Raleigh.

Q. What small Mississippi town was the only one displaced by construction of the Tennessee–Tombigbee Waterway?

A. Holcut.

Q. For what was Mills Darden, a resident of Henderson County in the 1840s and 50s, noted?

A. His size: 8 feet, 5 inches and weighing over 800 lbs.

Q. In what county in 1779 did Rev. Tidence Lane establish Buffalo Church, the first Baptist Church on Tennessee soil?

A. Washington County.

Q. What town is known as the "Mule Capital of the World"?

A. Columbia.

Q. The community of Skullbone is situated on the northeast edge of what county?

A. Gibson.

Q. Where is the Abraham Lincoln Museum featuring over 250,000 Lincoln and Civil War items located?

A. Harrogate.

Q. Originally called White's Landing, this Hardin County town was renamed in 1849 in honor of what decisive battle of the Mexican War?

A. Cerro Gordo.

Q. Where is the location of Loretta Lynn's Dude Ranch?

A. Hurricane Mills.

Q. Battle Ground Academy in Williamson County was originally founded in 1889 under what name?

A. Mooney & Wall School.

Q. In what county was the Hiwassee Copper Mine situated?

A. Polk County.

Q. Who was the resident of the Federal Soldier's Home at Johnson City who personally sprang the trap on sixty men while serving as executioner for the famous "Hanging Judge" Parker of Ft. Smith, Arkansas?

A. George Maledon.

Q. Box cars were built near what Loudon County town?

A. Lenoir City.

Q. Why was Crossville selected as the county seat of Cumberland County?

A. It was at the junction of the old Nashville-Knoxville Road and the Kentucky-Chattanooga Stock Road.

Q. Where is the largest automotive manufacturing plant under one roof in the United States?

A. Smyrna (Nissan).

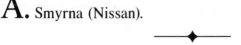

Q. In what county was the first federally-aided road project?

A. Hamilton County.

Q. What early pioneer trail serves at several points as the dividing line between Tennessee and North Carolina?

A. The Appalachian Trail.

Q. Where was Peter Turney, Confederate brigadier general, state supreme court chief justice and twice-elected governor, born?

A. Jasper, in Marion County.

Q. For what reason was a lady named Belle Seymour arrested in 1875 while standing at the corner of Main Street and Beale in Memphis?

A. For wearing pants.

Q. What city is known as "the Athens of the South"?

A. Nashville.

Q. A grouping of thirty-five prehistoric mounds and ancient fortifications in Madison County is presently known by what name?

A. Pinson Mounds.

Q. Auburntown, in Cannon County, has been known by what three other names?

A. Saunder's Fork, Poplar Stand and Auburn.

Q. Who served as the chairman of the Knoxville World's Fair Advisory Committee?

A. Jake Butcher.

Q. What is the physiographic region of Tennessee noted for its relatively flat-topped tablelands?

A. Cumberland Plateau.

Q. In what year did the first interstate section, consisting of 1.8 miles of I-65, open in Tennessee?

A. 1958.

Q. What is Nashville's sister city in Canada?

A. Edmonton.

Q. In what county was William Stone, who was presented a cane by the U. S. Congress for his bravery at Tippecanoe, born?

A. Sevier County.

Q. Where did the U. S. Navy have an inland shipbuilding and repair facility from 1844 to 1857?

A. At the mouth of the Wolf River on the Mississippi River.

Q. Who were the two largest landowners in the early 1800s in the Wolf River Valley area of Fentress County?

A. Conrad Pile, "Old Coonrod," great-great-grandfather of Alvin York, and John Clemens, father of Mark Twain.

Q. Where is the Tennessee Valley Railroad Museum?
A. Chattanooga.

Q. In what city is the Soybean Festival held?
A. Dyersburg.

Q. Who was the trapper and guide to the Rocky Mountains born in Roane County?

A. Joseph Rutherford Walker.

Q. The Lay Packing Company of Knoxville houses a machine that produces how many weiners in one hour?

A. 600,000.

Q. Who from Giles County was elected governor in 1870 and 1872?

A. John Calvin Brown.

Q. Many of the thriving nineteenth-century potteries in Middle Tennessee were in what three clay-rich counties?

A. DeKalb, White, and Putnam.

Q. What famous World War I hero's farm and grist mill is situated just north of Jamestown?

A. Alvin York.

Q. At what location in Anderson County in 1902 did one of America's worst mine disasters take place, killing 184 miners?

A. Fraterville Mine.

Q. What was the forerunner state that comprised much of which eventually became Tennessee?

A. The State of Franklin.

Q. Which two mountains rank second and third in elevation in the state?

A. Mt. Guyot (el. 6,621), and Mt. LeConte (el. 6,593).

Q. Which four Tennessee communities have the shortest names?

A. Arp, Fly, Fry and Una.

Q. Where is the geographic center of Tennessee, first determined in 1834?

A. Near Old Lascassas Pike, north of Murfreesboro.

Q. Where is the Davy Crockett tavern located?

A. Morristown.

Q. Carl Perkins, composer of *Blue Suede Shoes*, was born in 1932 near what town?

A. Tiptonville.

———◆———

Q. What city hosts the annual Tennessee State Fair?

A. Nashville.

———◆———

Q. What Chattanooga man was appointed first Postmaster General by President Benjamin Harrison?

A. H. Clay Evans.

———◆———

Q. Wilma Rudolph, Olympic track star, is a native of what city?

A. Clarksville.

———◆———

Q. How large is Tennessee in square miles?

A. 42,244, including inland waters.

———◆———

Q. Adelicia Hayes Franklin Acklen Cheatham was the mistress of what mansion and estate that became the social center of Nashville, the state, and much of the South?

A. Belmont.

———◆———

Q. Near what present-day town did the Cherokee Indians have a tollgate to exact tribute from pioneer travelers in the eighteenth century?

A. Rockwood.

Q. According to federal revenue officers, where in East Tennessee was one of the most active areas in producing moonshine in the nation?

A. Walden Ridge.

Q. Jackson, the geographic center of West Tennessee, has what nickname?

A. "Hub City."

Q. The breathtakingly beautiful Savage Gulf State Natural Area is found in what county?

A. Grundy County.

Q. What hamburger chain began in Chattanooga in 1932?

A. Krystal.

Q. Lovely City, the smallest incorporated town in Tennessee, was incorporated with how many qualified voters?

A. Seventeen.

Q. What restored Indian village in Memphis may have been occupied as early as 800 A.D.?

A. Chucalissa.

Q. What is the name of the national forest that stretches along the Tennessee-North Carolina border?

A. Cherokee National Forest.

Q. What city serves as the gateway to the Great Smoky Mountain National Park?

A. Gatlinburg.

Q. Where was the famous "Monkey Trial" held?

A. Dayton.

Q. The Great Revival movement, which started in Kentucky in 1860 and swept through Tennessee, had one of its most notable meetings at what location in Tennessee?

A. Drake's Creek.

Q. Moss Island State Waterfowl Refuge is located in what county?

A. Dyer County.

Q. Where is the Liberty Bowl held?

A. Memphis.

Q. In what year did the great Gay Street fire take place in Knoxville?

A. 1897.

Q. Who were the noted desperados who hid in the White's Creek area of Davidson County during the spring of 1881?

A. Jesse James and the James Gang.

Q. As a young man, where did President Andrew Johnson set up his very own tailoring business?

A. Rutledge.

Q. Tennessee is made up of how many counties?

A. 95.

Q. What Middle Tennessee community is the home of Castle Gwyn, modeled on a medieval Welsh castle?

A. Triune.

Q. What Tennessee city was first named Ross's Landing?

A. Chattanooga.

Q. For whom was the old Maxwell House Hotel in Nashville named?

A. Mary Maxwell Overton, the wife of its builder, John Overton.

Q. What city grew to a population of 75,000 within two years of its establishment?

A. Oak Ridge.

Q. What was the occupation of Thomas Edison while living in Memphis?

A. Telegraph operator.

Q. What is the name of the Cumberland County rehabilta-tion project administered by the Farm Security Adminis-tration for stranded families?

A. Cumberland Homesteads.

Q. What town is known as the "Phosphate Capital of the World"?

A. Mt. Pleasant.

Q. What legendary female country artist is one of the few entertainers born in Nashville?

A. Kitty Wells.

Q. Which lake is noted for its cypress boats and cypress trees?

A. Reelfoot Lake.

Q. The *Knoxville Gazette* was published for a short time in what town before moving to Knoxville proper?

A. Rogersville.

Q. What lake in DeKalb County is noted for its fishing depth and beauty?

A. Center Hill Reservoir.

Q. What county was devastated by the DeGraffenreid Storm in 1835?

A. Maury.

Q. Where was the last council meeting held between the United States and the Cherokee Nation preceding the removal of the Indians to Indian Territory?

A. Red Clay Council Ground, Bradley County.

Q. What was the first community on Lookout Mountain?

A. Summertown.

Q. What city is known as the "city of churches"?

A. Memphis.

Q. Which community in Hickman County had a large resort?

A. Bon Aqua.

Q. What European nation was the first to declare its participation in the Knoxville World's Fair?

A. Italy.

Q. Covering 43,000 acres, what is the largest state park?

A. Natchez Trace State Park.

Q. The underground lake known as the Lost Sea is located near what town?

A. Sweetwater.

Q. Which two rivers were the last stronghold of flatboating in the Tennessee River system?

A. The Clinch and Powell Rivers.

Q. On June 22, 1910, the world's first night airplane flight took off from what location?

A. Cumberland Park, Nashville.

Q. What road, when completed in 1820, cut 220 miles from the distance between Nashville and New Orleans when compared to previously existing roads?

A. Jackson's Military Road.

———◆———

Q. How many states may be viewed from Lookout Mountain?

A. Seven.

———◆———

Q. What present-day county courthouse is modeled after the Lincoln Memorial?

A. Carroll County Courthouse.

———◆———

Q. In what town did Alex Haley spend some of his early years?

A. Henning.

———◆———

Q. Famous female singer and television personality Dinah Shore is from what county?

A. Franklin County.

Q. What city is the trade center for the region consisting of western Tennessee, eastern Arkansas, northern Mississippi, northwestern Alabama, western Kentucky and southeastern Missouri?

A. Memphis.

Q. Where was Uncle Dave Macon born?

A. On a farm near Smart Station.

Q. What was the famous gateway to the west, situated south of Kingsport on the banks of the Holston River, called?

A. The Boat Yard.

Q. In what state historic area does the "eternal flame of the Cherokee Nation" burn?

A. Red Clay.

Q. Which Tennessee rivers enter the Ohio River near Paducah, Kentucky?

A. The Cumberland and Tennessee Rivers.

Q. What city in Tennessee has been called the "Atomic Bomb City"?

A. Oak Ridge.

Q. What was the name of the home of James Winchester, who helped found Memphis?

A. Cragfont, in Sumner County.

Q. What is the highest point of elevation in Tennessee?

A. Clingmans Dome, 6,643 feet (2,025 meters) above sea level.

Q. Where did Memphis get its name?

A. It was named for the ancient Egyptian capital of Memphis, which was on the banks of the Nile River.

Q. What are the two main tributaries of the Big South Fork of the Cumberland River?

A. Clear Fork and New River.

Q. What city has the largest population in the state?

A. Memphis.

Q. Into how many land regions is Tennessee divided?

A. Seven. The Blue Ridge, the Appalachian Ridge and Valley, the Appalachian Plateau or Cumberland Plateau, the Highland Rim, the Nashville Basin, the Gulf Coastal Plain, and the Mississippi Alluvial Plain.

Q. Where was the American statesman Cordell Hull born?

A. Overton County (now Pickett County).

Q. What was the first county seat of Humphreys County?

A. Reynoldsburg, 1812-1837.

Q. A boundary line running from the mouth of Cloud's Creek to the Cumberland Gap served what purpose under the 1777 Treaty of Long Island?

A. Dividing line between white settlements and Indian territories.

Q. Tennessee has how many airports?
A. About 125.

Q. Where is the Country Music Hall of Fame?
A. Nashville.

Q. Where does Tennessee rank in population compared to the other states?

A. Seventeenth.

Q. Davy Crockett was born near what present-day town?
A. Rogersville.

Q. Where is the W. B. Tanner Co. Inc., the world's largest producer of radio jingles, located?

A. Memphis.

Q. In what county was bluegrass musician Earl Scruggs born?

A. Overton County.

Q. The agricultural commune called the Farm, founded by Stephen Gaskin, is situated near what community?

A. Summertown.

Q. In what town does the character Minnie Pearl live?

A. Grinder's Switch.

Q. What town was a rival of Memphis for commercial supremacy in the 1820s and 30s?

A. Randolph.

Q. What states border Tennessee?

A. Alabama, Georgia, Mississippi, North Carolina, Kentucky, Virginia, Missouri and Arkansas.

Q. What is the fourth largest city in Tennessee?

A. Chattanooga.

Q. Land Between the Lakes is found between which two major lakes?

A. Kentucky Lake and Lake Barkley.

Q. Which Indian tribe lived in what is now the Memphis area?

A. The Chickasaw Indians.

Q. In what county is the David Crockett State Park?

A. Lawrence County.

◆

Q. Where was the first railroad bridge built across the Mississippi River, south of St. Louis?

A. Memphis, 1892.

◆

Q. Tennessee Meiji Gakuin, the first fully accredited Japanese high school in the United States, is in what town?

A. Sweetwater.

◆

Q. What Columbia resident was known as the "Fighting Bishop"?

A. Leonidas Polk.

◆

Q. In what park can be seen a portion of the "Great Indian Warpath"?

A. Reflection Riding.

◆

Q. Where is the "world's largest teapot collection"?

A. Trenton.

◆

Q. Who was the opera and concert singer born in Cocke County?

A. Grace Moore.

Q. How many farms operate in Tennessee, with 80 percent having under 180 acres?

A. 96,000.

Q. How many electoral votes are allocated to Tennessee?

A. Ten.

Q. The Foxfire Arts and Crafts Festival is held in what town?

A. Maryville.

Q. Which country music star has a street named in his honor in Hendersonville?

A. Johnny Cash.

Q. Which principal chief of the Cherokee Nation had his last home east of the Mississippi River in Bradley County?

A. Chief John Ross.

Q. Where was the first plow factory in the South?

A. Chattanooga.

Q. What do the three stars on the Tennessee state flag represent?

A. East, Middle and West Tennessee.

ENTERTAINMENT

C H A P T E R   T W O

Q. What record label in Memphis signed such greats as Elvis Presley, Jerry Lee Lewis, Carl Perkins, Roy Orbison, Johnny Cash and Charlie Rich in the early fifties?

A. Sun Records.

Q. What Nashville music artist has the distinction of having his records heard all the way to the moon?

A. Faron Young, when Pete Conrad carried his tapes with him on the Apollo 12 mission.

Q. For what song is Country Music Hall of Fame member Tex Ritter, probably best known?

A. *High Noon,* from the motion picture of the same name.

Q. What was Elvis Presley's first motion picture?

A. *Love Me Tender.*

Q. What was the name of Broadway's long-running comedy in which Nashville born actress, Barbara Coggins, starred?

A. *Gemini.*

Q. Country music stars, past and present, are honored at what building in Nashville?

A. Country Music Hall of Fame.

✦

Q. Who was the noted blues musician in Memphis who worked as a street cleaner by day?

A. Walter "Furry" Lewis.

✦

Q. What Nashville-based country music star was a member of Buddy Holly's band, the "Crickets"?

A. Waylon Jennings.

✦

Q. Who was known as the "Dixie Dewdrop" of the Grand Ole Opry?

A. Uncle Dave Macon.

✦

Q. What nationally renowned southern gospel group has worked out of Memphis for many years?

A. The Blackwood Brothers Quartet.

✦

Q. What Nashville native won an Oscar for his screenplay for *Dead Poets Society*?

A. Tom Schulman.

✦

Q. What man came to Fisk University interested in Sunday School work among the freedmen and gave his leisure time to instruct the pupils in vocal music?

A. George L. White, founder of the Jubilee Singers.

Q. What bass singer who has spent much of his career in Memphis and Nashville, sang with such gospel quartets as the Sunny South, Sunshine Boys, Blackwood Brothers, and Stamps, and toured with Elvis Presley, is known as the world's lowest bass singer?

A. J. D. Sumner.

◆

Q. What *Hee Haw* performer is known for the songs, *Mountain Dew* and *Old Rattler*?

A. Grandpa Jones.

◆

Q. What star of the television series "My Friend Flicka," and movies such as *The Steel Helmet* and *Walking Tall* is a resident of Jackson?

A. Gene Evans.

◆

Q. Whose parents forced him to exchange his new guitar for a dictionary?

A. W. C. Handy.

◆

Q. What Knoxville lady became well-known as an actress, singer, television star, founder and owner of her own cosmetics firm, film producer, and is on the board of the Singer Sewing Machine Company?

A. Polly Bergen.

◆

Q. What Grand Ole Opry personality was born in Ashland City in 1874?

A. Obed "Dad" Pickard.

◆

Q. Who is the only person with a mother, uncle, aunt and husband in the Country Music Hall of Fame?

A. June Carter.

Q. Who was the co-founder of one of Nashville's largest music publishing firms and wrote such hits as *Blue Eyes Crying in the Rain, Kaw-Liga,* and *Take These Chains From My Heart*?

A. Fred Rose.

———◆———

Q. The first National Quartet Convention was held in what city in 1956?

A. Memphis.

———◆———

Q. What is the name of the group, headquartered in Hendersonville, that began in gospel music and has evolved into one of the top country-pop groups in the nation with such hits as *Sail Away, The Y'all Come Back Saloon, Bobby Sue* and *Elvira*?

A. The Oak Ridge Boys.

———◆———

Q. What jazz bass player started a nationally recognized school of music in Nashville?

A. W. O. Smith.

———◆———

Q. When Loretta Lynn made her first appearance on the Grand Ole Opry in 1960, she performed what song?

A. *Honky Tonk Girl.*

———◆———

Q. On what occasion was a trumpet first used on the Grand Ole Opry?

A. *Taps* was played on the occasion of President Franklin Roosevelt's death, at the suggestion of Pee Wee King.

———◆———

Q. What country entertainer has traveled the most miles?

A. Ernest Tubb.

Q. What famous black harmonica player performed in the early days of the Grand Ole Opry?

A. Deford Bailey.

Q. The proceeds from the first concert of the newly-organized Fisk University Jubilee Singers were donated to aid victims of which great urban disaster?

A. The Great Chicago Fire.

Q. Who is known as the "Tennessee Plow Boy"?

A. Eddy Arnold.

Q. What country music performer spent almost ten years in Nashville trying to make it in the entertainment business, only to become a star after returning to Texas?

A. Willie Nelson.

Q. What is the price on the tag of Minnie Pearl's hat?

A. $1.98.

Q. What Tennessee filmmaker won an Oscar for his documentary about Frederic Remington?

A. Tom Neff.

Q. Grand Ole Opry star Jean Shepherd was married to what performer who was killed in the plane crash along with Patsy Cline and Cowboy Copas?

A. Hawkshaw Hawkins.

Q. Francis Robinson, remembered as assistant manager of the Metropolitan Opera and for writing the biography of Enrico Caruso, was an usher in what Nashville auditorium?

A. The Ryman Auditorium.

Q. What political office did Woodward Maurice "Tex" Ritter seek in 1970?

A. United States Senator.

Q. What Nashville-born actor had roles on the *Daniel Boone Show* and *The Virginian* and sang with the Kingston Trio and the New Christy Minstrels?

A. Dave Peel.

Q. Where can you see Elvis Presley's 1960 "Solid Gold Cadillac"?

A. The Country Music Hall of Fame and Museum.

Q. What entertainer starred on the Grand Ole Opry for many years and emceed his own show on ABC-TV, *Jubilee USA*?

A. Red Foley.

Q. What star of *The Lords of Discipline* can often be found on the sidelines with the University of Tennessee Vols?

A. David Keith.

Q. What radio station in Knoxville was the starting place for many country performers?

A. WNOX.

Q. What was one of the very first country albums to be a million-seller?

A. *Johnny Cash At Folsom Prison.*

———◆———

Q. "The Knoxville Girl" was the American version of what English ballad?

A. "The Berkshire Tragedy."

———◆———

Q. The Blackwood Brothers Quartet of Memphis were the first gospel group to utilize a bus for concert tour transportation and the first gospel group to record for which major label?

A. RCA.

———◆———

Q. What Nashville session guitarist has played on dozens of hit records, and gained fame of his own by recording *Gotta Travel On* in 1959?

A. Billy Grammer.

———◆———

Q. How much ground does Opryland USA cover?

A. 120 acres.

———◆———

Q. What 50,000-watt station broadcasts the Grand Ole Opry?

A. WSM Radio.

———◆———

Q. What was the name of the famous country music touring group that performed for United States Service personnel around the world during World War II?

A. The Grand Ole Opry Camel Caravan.

Q. What McMinnville-born star joined the Grand Ole Opry in 1964 and has had many successful recordings with Kenny Rogers?

A. Dottie West.

———◆———

Q. What famous Knoxville theater opened in 1909, hosted many famous stars, and currently serves the community as a performing arts center?

A. The Bijou.

———◆———

Q. Why did Elvis Presley write the Memphis draft board requesting a delay in being drafted?

A. So he could finish the film *King Creole*, already in production. He requested the delay not for himself, but for the film company, because it would lose a great deal of money. The request was granted.

———◆———

Q. Adger M. Pace, working with the Vaughan Publishing Company in Lawrenceburg, organized what musical event?

A. The National Singing Convention.

———◆———

Q. Jerry Lee Lewis made his Opry debut in 1973 and during his performance asked what Opry regular to join him on stage?

A. Del Wood, piano player.

———◆———

Q. What Tennessee group joined the Marshall Tucker Band, James Talley and Guy Lombardo in performing at Jimmy Carter's 1977 Inauguration Ball?

A. The Charlie Daniels Band.

———◆———

Q. For what man was the Ryman Auditorium originally built?

A. The great revivalist, Sam Jones.

Q. Who was the Clarksville-born actor who starred as "Sergeant Carter" in the mid-60s hit television series *Gomer Pyle USMC*?

A. Frank Spencer Sutton.

———◆———

Q. When Tennessee governor Frank Clement was brought to the platform to make the keynote speech at the 1956 Democratic Convention, what song was played?

A. *The Tennessee Waltz.*

———◆———

Q. What was the most famous of all Beale Street establishments?

A. Peewee's Place.

———◆———

Q. In what science fiction farce did Jim Varney, best known for playing Ernest P. Worrell, portray at least five characters?

A. *Dr. Otto and the Riddle of the Gloom Beam.*

———◆———

Q. Who was Tennessee's first professional actress?

A. Mrs. Mary Squires of Franklin.

———◆———

Q. Where was Tex Ritter when he died of a heart attack in 1974?

A. Nashville's Metro jail, where he was trying to arrange bail for one of his band members.

———◆———

Q. What is the name of the longest-running radio show in history?

A. The Grand Ole Opry.

Q. What United States President appeared on stage during opening ceremonies of the new Grand Ole Opry House?

A. Richard M. Nixon.

Q. What song is considered to be the Carter Family theme song?

A. *Keep on the Sunny Side.*

Q. What legendary Opry entertainer was known as the "Texas Troubadour"?

A. Ernest Tubb.

Q. What date marked the last performance of the Grand Ole Opry in the Ryman Auditorium?

A. March 15, 1974.

Q. Who was known for truck driving songs such as *Teddy Bear, Giddyup Go* and *Phantom 309*?

A. Red Sovine.

Q. How many movies did Elvis Presley make?

A. 32.

Q. What nationally acclaimed Knoxville actress, in the space of five years, saw her baby son critically injured in a car accident, watched her oldest daughter die from inflammation of the brain, and herself suffered three massive strokes?

A. Patricia Neal.

Q. Who is the country music performer who, along with Jessi Colter, Willie Nelson, Tompall Glaser and his band, became known as the Outlaws?

A. Waylon Jennings.

Q. In the long history of the Grand Ole Opry, what entertainer holds the record for encores?

A. Hank Williams, singing *Lovesick Blues,* 6 encores.

Q. What famous country song has been recorded over a thousand times?

A. *Rocky Top.*

Q. What company did Elvis Presley work for after his graduation from high school?

A. Crown Electric Company in Memphis, as a truck driver.

Q. Who is the writer of such hit songs as *Waterloo, Long Black Veil, PT-109,* and *One Day at a Time,* who has been called the Den Mother of Nashville because of her willingness to help struggling musicians?

A. Marijohn Wilkin.

Q. What nationally known promoter of gospel and country music organized the first all-night sing in the Ryman Auditorium on November 8, 1948?

A. Wally Fowler.

Q. What two radio programs on WNOX in Knoxville helped the growth of bluegrass and country music in that area?

A. *Mid-Day Merry-Go-Round* and *The Tennessee Barn Dance.*

Q. Who wrote the hit song *Sixteen Tons* for singer Tennessee Ernie Ford?

A. Merle Travis.

———◆———

Q. In 1925 WSM went on the air as a 1,000-watt channel, the broadcasting station of National Life and Accident Insurance Company, and introduced a hillbilly show by what name?

A. WSM Barn Dance.

———◆———

Q. Who performed the theme song for the movie *Bonnie and Clyde*?

A. Lester Flatt and Earl Scruggs, *Foggy Mountain Breakdown*.

———◆———

Q. What famous country star has created a foundation for child abuse?

A. Hank Snow, who was an abused child.

———◆———

Q. Who is the country music entertainer known for his guitar-shaped swimming pool?

A. Webb Pierce.

———◆———

Q. How did the tag "The Solemn Old Judge" become associated with George D. Hay?

A. "The Solemn Old Judge" was the title of a newspaper column he had written during his newspaper days.

———◆———

Q. From what high school did Elvis graduate in 1953?

A. Humes High School, Memphis.

Q. In what year was the Grand Ole Opry radio program first aired?

A. 1925.

————◆————

Q. What was Ronnie Milsap's first job after moving from Memphis to Nashville?

A. Playing at Roger Miller's King of the Road Motel.

————◆————

Q. Who brought the Swedish Nightingale Jenny Lind to Nashville during her United States tour of 1850-52?

A. P. T. Barnum.

————◆————

Q. When was the Country Music Association in Nashville founded?

A. 1965.

————◆————

Q. A country show at the Overton Park Shell in Memphis featured Webb Pierce, Slim Whitman and Marty Robbins, but what other young, up-and-coming entertainer stole the show?

A. Elvis Presley, who had been added to the bill at the last minute.

————◆————

Q. What Donelson native wrote and directed *Liar's Moon* starring Matt Dillon?

A. David Fisher.

————◆————

Q. What is the name of the attraction in Sevier county containing thirty-five scenes featuring lifelike personalities from movies, TV and country music?

A. Stars Over Gatlinburg.

Q. Who is the younger sister of Loretta Lynn and a super country-pop star in her own right?

A. Crystal Gayle.

Q. Who were the first performers to record successful country music records in Tennessee?

A. The Carter Family and Jimmie Rodgers, in Bristol.

Q. Born in Cocke County in 1901, what was Grace Moore noted for?

A. She was one of the outstanding operatic sopranos of her day.

Q. What great country star was known as "Gentleman Jim"?

A. Jim Reeves.

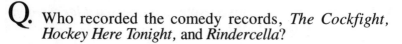

Q. What country music star has made several appearances on the daytime soap opera, *One Life to Live*?

A. Bill Anderson.

Q. Who recorded the comedy records, *The Cockfight, Hockey Here Tonight,* and *Rindercella*?

A. Archie Campbell.

Q. Anita Kerr, organizer of the Anita Kerr Singers, was born in what city?

A. Memphis.

Q. What musician was named "Outstanding Instrumentalist" by *Cash Box Magazine,* fourteen years in a row?

A. Chet Atkins.

Q. What year did Roy Acuff run for governor of Tennessee on the Republican ticket?

A. 1948, defeated by Democrat Gordon Browning.

Q. In what movie did Claude Jarman, Jr., child actor from Nashville, star with Gregory Peck in 1947?

A. *The Yearling.*

Q. What high school did Dinah Shore, singer and television personality, attend?

A. Hume-Fogg High School, Nashville.

Q. What was Barbara Mandrell's first Number One record?

A. *Sleeping Single in a Double Bed.*

Q. Who is the former wife of Kris Kristofferson who lived in Nashville as a girl while her father pastored churches in the area?

A. Rita Coolidge.

Q. What famous musician composed the *Beale Street Blues*?

A. W. C. Handy.

Q. What entertainers had two recording sessions in WSM's Studio B that were said to be the beginning of the Nashville recording industry?

A. Red Foley in 1945, and later that same year, Ernest Tubb.

Q. What song by Lester Flatt was Number One on the country music charts for three months in 1962?

A. *Ballad of Jed Clampett.*

Q. What year was the Grand Ole Opry televised for the first time?

A. 1950.

Q. Who was Crossville's great gift to Hollywood?

A. Marjorie Weaver.

Q. When Johnny Cash performed his first free concert for the San Quentin Prison inmates on January 1, 1960, what inmate who was at the concert later became a country music star?

A. Merle Haggard.

Q. What Nashville session musician became famous for his recording *Last Date*?

A. Floyd Cramer.

Q. What television personality, known for hosting game shows, is from Jackson?

A. Wink Martindale.

Q. Who is the personality from Nashville noted for his zany roles in radio and television commercials?

A. Jim Varney (Ernest P. Worrell).

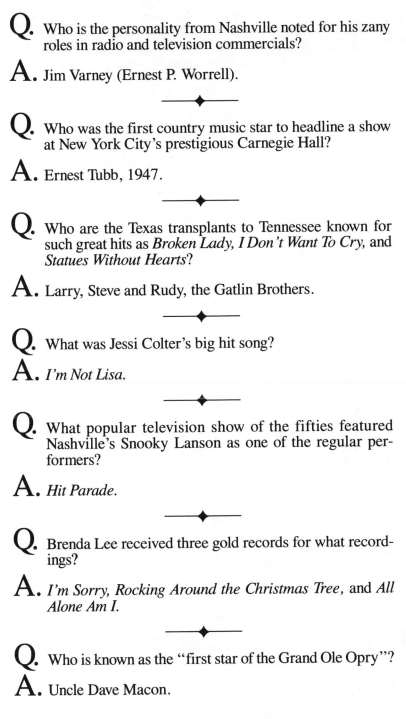

Q. Who was the first country music star to headline a show at New York City's prestigious Carnegie Hall?

A. Ernest Tubb, 1947.

Q. Who are the Texas transplants to Tennessee known for such great hits as *Broken Lady, I Don't Want To Cry,* and *Statues Without Hearts*?

A. Larry, Steve and Rudy, the Gatlin Brothers.

Q. What was Jessi Colter's big hit song?

A. *I'm Not Lisa.*

Q. What popular television show of the fifties featured Nashville's Snooky Lanson as one of the regular performers?

A. *Hit Parade.*

Q. Brenda Lee received three gold records for what recordings?

A. *I'm Sorry, Rocking Around the Christmas Tree,* and *All Alone Am I.*

Q. Who is known as the "first star of the Grand Ole Opry"?

A. Uncle Dave Macon.

Q. What entertainer, born in Tennessee lost his father on his eleventh birthday and that same year his family lost their farm, only to become sharecroppers on the same land?

A. Eddy Arnold.

Q. What was the original name of the Ryman Auditorium?

A. The Union Gospel Tabernacle.

Q. Who is the dynamic rhythm and blues, rock-n-roll queen born in Brownsville on November 26, 1938?

A. Tina Turner.

Q. In what year was the first country music show on Broadway, featuring Roy Acuff, Kitty Wells, and Johnny and Jack?

A. 1957, at the Palace Theater.

Q. What is Minnie Pearl's real name?

A. Sarah Ophelia Cannon.

Q. Which Grand Ole Opry star was known for such hits as *Candy Kisses* and *In the Misty Moonlight*?

A. George Morgan.

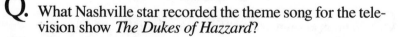

Q. What Nashville star recorded the theme song for the television show *The Dukes of Hazzard*?

A. Waylon Jennings.

Q. When was the excellent and popular Staub's Theater opened in Knoxville?

A. October 1, 1872.

———◆———

Q. Barbara Mandrell plays how many instruments in her act?

A. Four: pedal steel guitar, 5-string banjo, saxophone and bass guitar.

———◆———

Q. Who is known as the "Queen of Country Music"?

A. Miss Kitty Wells.

———◆———

Q. What soul/gospel singer of Memphis started Full Gospel Tabernacle in 1976?

A. Al Green.

———◆———

Q. What is the name of Dolly Parton's family theme park in Pigeon Forge?

A. Dollywood.

———◆———

Q. Who was the actor and later famous assassin who appeared February 1-6, 1864, at the Nashville Theater?

A. John Wilkes Booth.

———◆———

Q. Who from Jellico sang in Irving Berlin's *Music Box Review*, was a member of the Metropolitan Opera Company and starred in the motion pictures *New Moon* and *Jenny Lind*?

A. Grace Moore.

Q. What was the name of the hit motion picture for which Dolly Parton composed and performed the theme song and starred with Lillie Tomlin and Jane Fonda?

A. *9 to 5.*

Q. Who is the country music entertainer well-known for his super hit *Waterloo* and shares the same name as a great Confederate general?

A. Stonewall Jackson.

Q. What Tennessee-born entertainer was the voice for Baloo the Bear in Walt Disney's *Jungle Book*?

A. Phil Harris.

Q. In what movie did country picker Jerry Reed make his directorial debut?

A. *What Comes Around.*

Q. How many seats did the Ryman Auditorium contain?

A. Thirty-three hundred.

Q. *Living Proof,* the made-for-television movie shot in Middle Tennessee, was based on the life of which country music entertainer?

A. Hank Williams, Jr.

Q. Where is the Jim Reeves Museum?

A. *Evergreen Place,* Nashville.

Q. The country music attractions called *Twitty City* and *Music City U.S.A.* are found in what town?

A. Hendersonville.

Q. What was the first duet hit recorded by Dolly Parton and Porter Wagoner?

A. *The Last Thing On My Mind.*

Q. The Jackson Area Plectral Society is dedicated to preserving what type of music?

A. Old-time string music.

Q. What Tennessee entertainer did *Time* magazine recognize as "the Country Como"?

A. Eddy Arnold.

Q. What is the name of Roy Acuff's band?

A. Smoky Mountain Boys.

Q. Ed Bruce, Nashville singer and songwriter, was a regular on what television show starring James Garner?

A. *Maverick.*

Q. What country entertainer used the name Simon Crum for his comedy routines?

A. Ferlin Husky.

Q. Del Wood, famous piano player on the Grand Ole Opry, was noted for what big hit?

A. *Down Yonder.*

Q. What was Dinah Shore's given name?

A. Rose.

Q. Carl Smith and Goldie Hill, married in 1957, live on a large ranch in what town?

A. Franklin.

Q. Who was the famous female Beale Street performer known best for her hit *Am I Blue*?

A. Ethel Waters.

Q. What was the first gospel music publishing company to back and promote southern gospel quartets?

A. The Vaughan Publishing Company of Lawrenceburg.

Q. Who is known as the "First Lady of Country Music"?

A. Tammy Wynette.

Q. What major record label was first to locate its country music division in Nashville?

A. Capitol Records, followed closely by Mercury Records.

Q. What entertainer hosts the Volunteer Jam each January in Nashville?

A. Charlie Daniels.

Q. Where is the Elvis Hall of Fame featuring more than 100 personal items of the "King of Rock and Roll" located?

A. Gatlinburg.

Q. To what did the term "Midnight Ramble" refer?

A. An added showing starting an hour before midnight on Thursday evening, for whites to come to the Beale Street Palace and see a performance of that week's shows.

Q. What renowned Opry star died January 1, 1953?

A. Hank Williams.

Q. In what year did Opryland USA open?

A. 1972.

Q. What film starring Matthew Modine was about the first B-17 to complete twenty-five combat missions during World War II?

A. *Memphis Belle.*

Q. Who renamed the WSM Barn Dance the Grand Ole Opry?

A. The Solemn Old Judge, George D. Hay.

Q. Who is the country music performer who moved to Nashville in 1962 and in 1974 had a giant single called *Country Bumpkin*?

A. Cal Smith.

Q. Sparta is noted for being the hometown of what great bluegrass picker?

A. Lester Flatt.

Q. *Hot Buttered Soul,* which had a tremendous effect on the course of black music and pop music in general, was recorded by what great black musician and singer born in Covington?

A. Isaac Hayes.

Q. What was the name of Uncle Dave Macon's band?

A. The Fruit Jar Drinkers.

Q. What is the name of Ernest Tubb's son, also a Grand Ole Opry member?

A. Justin Tubb.

Q. How old was Brenda Lee when she made her debut in the country charts?

A. Twelve years old.

Q. What country performer was the first to use a modern vocal group back-up?

A. Ferlin Husky, with the song *Gone*.

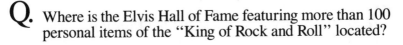

Q. Who were Johnny Cash's back-up musicians, known as the "Tennessee Two"?

A. Luther Perkins and Marshall Grant.

———◆———

Q. Who was the two-time Academy Award-winning actor who lived in Nashville as a child while his father taught music at Ward-Belmont College?

A. Melvyn Edouard "Melvyn Douglas" Hesselberg.

———◆———

Q. What child actor from Williamson County has appeared in *Barnum, The Nerd,* and on the television series "Elvis"?

A. Trevor Haley.

———◆———

Q. What television personality born in Winchester had polio as a baby?

A. Dinah Shore.

———◆———

Q. What country music performer is known as the "Singing Ranger"?

A. Hank Snow.

———◆———

Q. What young man moved to Nashville at age 3, grew up to be a teenage idol who sold more than 50 million records, earned 13 gold discs, 2 gold albums and a platinum album (having 3 million in sales), had his own television show, and starred in 15 motion pictures?

A. Pat Boone.

———◆———

Q. Iron City-born Melba Montgomery teamed with which country music legend to record several Top Ten hits during the 1960s?

A. George Jones.

Q. Who was the first non-performer named to the Country Music Hall of Fame?

A. James R. Denney, renowned talent promoter.

Q. What Chattanooga building houses a concert hall for blues and jazz?

A. The Bessie Smith Performance Hall.

Q. Who was the Knox County Court judge who wrote the opera, *The Story of Esther*?

A. Julius Ochs.

Q. What musician is known as "Mr. Nashville"?

A. Chet Atkins.

Q. Who was the first female elected to the Country Music Hall of Fame?

A. Patsy Cline.

Q. What Nashville female country singer gained fame by being a regular on the Lawrence Welk Show?

A. Lynn Anderson.

Q. What was the real name of the Grand Ole Opry comedian "The Duke of Paducah"?

A. Whitey Ford.

Q. What was the original name of W. C. Handy's *Memphis Blues*?

A. *Mr. Crump Don't 'Low.*

Q. What structure in Tennessee is the world's largest broadcast studio?

A. The Grand Ole Opry House.

Q. What performer holds the title, "King of Country Music"?

A. Roy Acuff.

Q. What was the first song Johnny Cash recorded that broke into the country charts?

A. *Cry, Cry, Cry.*

Q. What Nashville university boasts the Jubilee Singers, who immortalized the Negro spiritual and performed before kings, queens and other dignitaries?

A. Fisk University.

Q. Where were the first two successful recordings of country music made?

A. Bristol, 1927.

Q. What famous singer took Tennessee for his first name?

A. Tennessee Ernie Ford.

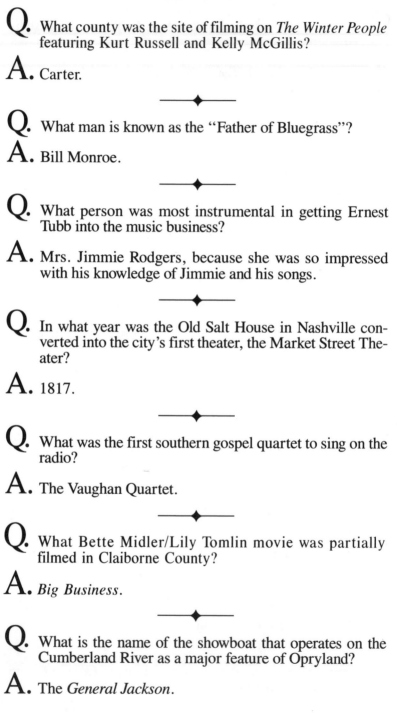

Q. What county was the site of filming on *The Winter People* featuring Kurt Russell and Kelly McGillis?

A. Carter.

Q. What man is known as the "Father of Bluegrass"?

A. Bill Monroe.

Q. What person was most instrumental in getting Ernest Tubb into the music business?

A. Mrs. Jimmie Rodgers, because she was so impressed with his knowledge of Jimmie and his songs.

Q. In what year was the Old Salt House in Nashville converted into the city's first theater, the Market Street Theater?

A. 1817.

Q. What was the first southern gospel quartet to sing on the radio?

A. The Vaughan Quartet.

Q. What Bette Midler/Lily Tomlin movie was partially filmed in Claiborne County?

A. *Big Business*.

Q. What is the name of the showboat that operates on the Cumberland River as a major feature of Opryland?

A. The *General Jackson*.

Q. W. C. Handy's *St. Louis Blues* was written in what establishment?

A. At the cigar stand in Peewee's Place, Memphis.

Q. Who founded Sun Records of Memphis?

A. Sam Phillips.

Q. The Gospel Music Association, headquartered in Nashville, was founded in what year?

A. 1964.

Q. Which country music entertainer owned the black limousine, called the longest in the world when built, formerly used by Jake Butcher in his unsuccessful bid for the governorship of Tennessee?

A. Tom T. Hall.

Q. When the Country Music Hall of Fame began, there was a total agreement that what person would be the first to be honored?

A. Jimmie Rodgers.

Q. What was the date of Nashville's first recording session?

A. September 28, 1928, in the YMCA hall.

Q. What recording artist had the biggest hit records on the Sun label?

A. Jerry Lee Lewis, *Whole Lot of Shakin' Goin' On* and *Great Balls of Fire*.

Q. Two-thirds of what 1984 movie starring Jeff Bridges was shot in Tennessee?

A. *Starman.*

Q. *Yakety Sax* brought what Nashville saxophone player to national fame?

A. Boots Randolph.

Q. What is the name of the longest running syndicated country comedy television show?

A. *Hee Haw.*

Q. What is the real name of country music singer Skeeter Davis of Brentwood?

A. Mary Frances Penick.

Q. Portions of which Clint Eastwood movie were shot in Tennessee?

A. *Honky Tonk Man.*

Q. What male quartet is featured on the Grand Ole Opry?

A. The Four Guys.

Q. Who is the young male performer who has done much to restore and preserve the traditional sounds of country music?

A. Ricky Skaggs.

HISTORY

CHAPTER THREE

Q. Which town in Roane County was the state capital for one day on September 21, 1807?

A. Kingston.

Q. Andrew Jackson became a national hero when he led his United States forces against the British in what battle?

A. The Battle of New Orleans.

Q. Who led the first European expedition into the Tennessee region?

A. Hernando de Soto, 1540.

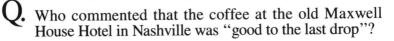

Q. Which notorious outlaws teamed up to form a wild west show that toured Tennessee in 1903?

A. Thomas Coleman Younger and Frank James.

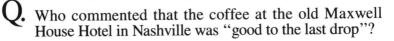

Q. Who commented that the coffee at the old Maxwell House Hotel in Nashville was "good to the last drop"?

A. Theodore Roosevelt.

Q. What was the name of the flatboat on which John Donelson came to Nashville?

A. *The Adventure.*

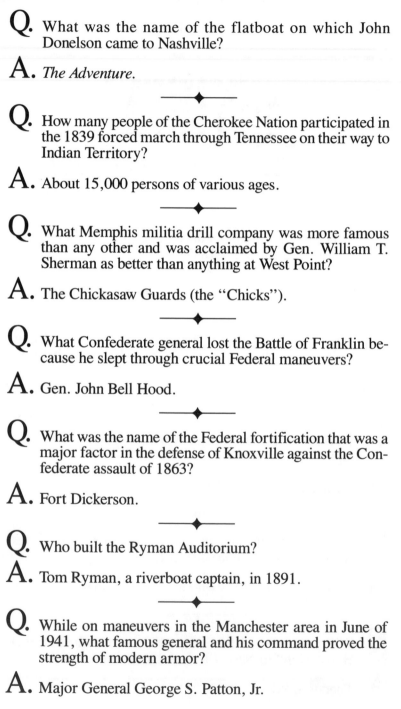

Q. How many people of the Cherokee Nation participated in the 1839 forced march through Tennessee on their way to Indian Territory?

A. About 15,000 persons of various ages.

Q. What Memphis militia drill company was more famous than any other and was acclaimed by Gen. William T. Sherman as better than anything at West Point?

A. The Chickasaw Guards (the "Chicks").

Q. What Confederate general lost the Battle of Franklin because he slept through crucial Federal maneuvers?

A. Gen. John Bell Hood.

Q. What was the name of the Federal fortification that was a major factor in the defense of Knoxville against the Confederate assault of 1863?

A. Fort Dickerson.

Q. Who built the Ryman Auditorium?

A. Tom Ryman, a riverboat captain, in 1891.

Q. While on maneuvers in the Manchester area in June of 1941, what famous general and his command proved the strength of modern armor?

A. Major General George S. Patton, Jr.

Q. What living history museum carries the original name of Murfreesboro?

A. Cannonsburgh.

———◆———

Q. By what other name was the Civil War Battle of Shiloh known?

A. The Battle of Pittsburg Landing.

———◆———

Q. Nashville was founded on what date?

A. Christmas day in 1779.

———◆———

Q. On what mountain did the "Last Battle of the Revolutionary War," fought a year after Cornwallis surrendered to George Washington, take place?

A. Lookout.

———◆———

Q. When did the last stagecoach holdup take place in Tennessee?

A. October 15, 1882.

———◆———

Q. What was the first railroad line in the state?

A. The LaGrange and Memphis.

———◆———

Q. Who in 1820 founded the Antiquarian Society, the forerunner of the Tennessee Historical Society?

A. John Haywood.

Q. Who was the Pickett County-born recipient of the Nobel Peace Prize for his efforts on behalf of the United Nations?

A. Cordell Hull.

Q. What was the name of the airfield from which air mail service was inaugurated from Nashville to Chicago in 1924?

A. Blackwood Field.

Q. What special event took place on June 8, 1861?

A. Tennessee seceded from the Union and joined the Confederacy.

Q. What is the name of the unusual prehistoric fortifications near Manchester?

A. Old Stone Fort.

Q. To whom did the English grant the region of Tennessee?

A. Sir Walter Raleigh, 1584.

Q. What were the combined casualties of the Battle at Shiloh during the War Between the States?

A. 23,500 killed in two days of fighting.

Q. What was the name of the locomotive Andrew's Raiders captured on April 12, 1862, in an attempt to cut Confederate communications between Chattanooga and Atlanta?

A. The General.

Q. Who was the transplanted New England sea captain who gave his flag, called "Old Glory," to occupying Union forces to fly above the state capitol building?

A. William Driver.

Q. What major Indian tribes lived in the Tennessee land area?

A. Cherokee, Chickamauga, Chickasaw and Iroquois.

Q. Who was the Scottish spinster heiress who founded a co-operative living colony near Nashoba in 1827?

A. Frances Wright.

Q. Who was the well-known Western gunfighter born in Clifton?

A. Robert Clay Allison.

Q. What means of conveyance was used to carry mail for two miles from Nashville on July 17, 1877?

A. The balloon, *Buffalo*.

Q. When did the Kentucky-Alabama Road first open through Tennessee?

A. 1806.

Q. Where was the Ku Klux Klan organized in 1855?

A. Pulaski, by Judge T. M. Jones and his son Calvin.

Q. The Department of the Interior was established in 1849 on the last day of what president's term in office?

A. James K. Polk.

———◆———

Q. Who was Tennessee's first governor?

A. John Sevier.

———◆———

Q. The first traffic-related law in the Tennessee Public Acts of 1837-38 stated that a driver should do what?

A. Drive to the right of the center of the road.

———◆———

Q. When were the first scheduled airline operations inaugurated in Tennessee?

A. December 1, 1925, between Atlanta and Evansville by way of Chattanooga and Louisville.

———◆———

Q. Who established a French trading post near present-day Nashville, in 1714?

A. Charles Charleville.

———◆———

Q. What year did Howard Baker become United States Senate minority leader?

A. 1977.

———◆———

Q. Under whose governorship was the state's first sales tax program passed into law?

A. Jim Nance McCord, 1945-1949.

Q. Who became the first female state trooper, joining the force in 1973?

A. Billie Jo Meeks.

◆

Q. What was the name of the mansion built in Memphis by Clarence Saunders, supermarket owner?

A. Pink Palace.

◆

Q. In what year did Robert Cavalier, Sieur de la Salle, claim Tennessee for France?

A. 1682.

◆

Q. What noted Methodist bishop held annual conferences in the home of William Nelson of Washington County in 1793, 1796 and 1797?

A. Francis Asbury.

◆

Q. What was the name of the black engine wiper who worked in the roundhouse in Jackson and immortalized Casey Jones in a folk song?

A. Wallace Saunders.

◆

Q. How many Republican governors has Tennessee elected in the twentieth century?

A. Four (Ben Hooper, Alfred Taylor, Winfield Dunn, Lamar Alexander).

◆

Q. David Crockett failed in a scheme to cut a canal between which two rivers?

A. The Hatchie and the Tennessee.

Q. What former Iranian hostage now sells U.S. flags in Franklin?

A. Jerry L. Boss.

Q. When was the earliest known wagon road built into the state, running between Burke County, North Carolina, and Jonesborough?

A. 1778.

Q. Who was the famous Confederate spy who lived near Smyrna?

A. Sam Davis.

Q. What supermarket chain was pioneered by Clarence Saunders of Memphis?

A. Piggly Wiggly, now owned by Kroger.

Q. What was the name of the only full-sized ship ever built for the United States Navy in Tennessee?

A. USS *Allegheny.*

Q. Alfred Alexander Taylor, defeated by his brother in the gubernatorial race of 1886, was finally elected governor in what year?

A. 1920.

Q. What three men organized a settlement in 1819 and named it Memphis?

A. Andrew Jackson, Judge John Overton and Gen. James Winchester.

Q. When was the Nashville, Chattanooga & St. Louis Railway completed?

A. 1854.

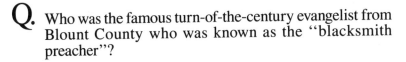

Q. Who was the famous turn-of-the-century evangelist from Blount County who was known as the "blacksmith preacher"?

A. Rev. J. T. "Tom" Sexton.

Q. Who was the first Whig governor of Tennessee?

A. Newton Cannon.

Q. Who was the five-term mayor of Memphis who served as United States Factor for the Chickasaw Indians from 1814 to 1818?

A. Isaac Rawlings.

Q. What did the Cherokees call themselves?

A. Ani-Yumoiva, or "principal (important) people."

Q. On what date was Sumner County created?

A. November 18, 1766.

Q. What former governor was nominated for U.S. Secretary of Education in 1990?

A. Lamar Alexander.

Q. What two pioneers braved the dangers of a new land and built Fort Nashborough, which later became Nashville?

A. James Robertson and John Donelson.

———◆———

Q. The Avery Treaty of June 20, 1777, was between white settlers and which Indian tribe?

A. Cherokee.

———◆———

Q. Who founded the first permanent Baptist church in Tennessee and served as moderator at the first Baptist Association meeting held in the state?

A. Tidence Lane.

———◆———

Q. What alias did Frank James, of the infamous James Gang, use while living in the Bordeaux area of Nashville?

A. Ben J. Woodson.

———◆———

Q. What man in 1970 became the first Republican in 50 years to be elected governor of Tennessee?

A. Winfield Dunn.

———◆———

Q. What is the name of Andrew Jackson's famous home?

A. The Hermitage.

———◆———

Q. What castle did Arthur Handly Marks, son of Tennessee's twenty-first governor Alfred S. Marks, build in Winchester in 1891?

A. Hundred Oaks Castle.

Q. What two cities other than Nashville have served for extended time periods as Tennessee capitals?

A. Knoxville (1792-1812, 1817) and Murfreesboro (1818-1826).

Q. When was the University of the South founded at Sewanee?

A. January 6, 1858.

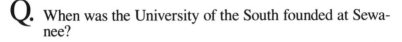

Q. What famous hotel in Chattanooga was built at the site of the Crutchfield House, destroyed by fire in 1867?

A. The Read House.

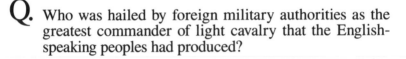

Q. Who was hailed by foreign military authorities as the greatest commander of light cavalry that the English-speaking peoples had produced?

A. Confederate General Nathan Bedford Forrest.

Q. What town based on old Quaker traditions was settled around 1796 by a few families of the Society of Friends?

A. Friendsville.

Q. What was the name of the first steamboat to reach Knoxville in March of 1828?

A. *The Atlas.*

Q. What is the name of the Nashville home of Judge John Overton, who helped found Memphis?

A. Traveller's Rest.

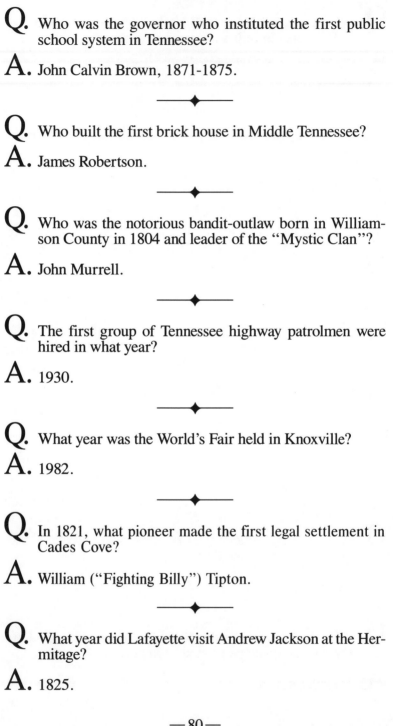

Q. Who was the governor who instituted the first public school system in Tennessee?

A. John Calvin Brown, 1871-1875.

———◆———

Q. Who built the first brick house in Middle Tennessee?

A. James Robertson.

———◆———

Q. Who was the notorious bandit-outlaw born in Williamson County in 1804 and leader of the "Mystic Clan"?

A. John Murrell.

———◆———

Q. The first group of Tennessee highway patrolmen were hired in what year?

A. 1930.

———◆———

Q. What year was the World's Fair held in Knoxville?

A. 1982.

———◆———

Q. In 1821, what pioneer made the first legal settlement in Cades Cove?

A. William ("Fighting Billy") Tipton.

———◆———

Q. What year did Lafayette visit Andrew Jackson at the Hermitage?

A. 1825.

Q. Near what Williamson County landmark is the only privately owned and maintained Civil War cemetery in the nation?

A. Carnton Mansion.

Q. The University of Tennessee at Martin was first established in 1900 under what name?

A. Hall-Moody College.

Q. How much was Joseph Terry, the builder of the first log courthouse in White County, paid for his services?

A. $25.00.

Q. Who was the Indian leader who protested the sale of Cherokee lands to the Transylvania Land Company in 1775 and led terrorist attacks against white settlers?

A. Tsu-gun-sini or Dragging Canoe.

Q. Columbia is on land that was part of a grant to what Revolutionary War colonel?

A. Nicholas Long.

Q. What flamboyant and unpredictable Tennessee judge stirred a wave of controversy in 1976 when he sent a fan letter to a pornographic magazine on official Tennessee Court of Criminal Appeals stationery?

A. Charles F. Galbreath.

Q. What bill was passed by the Tennessee General Assembly in 1875, providing state assistance for the construction of private schools, academies and institutions?

A. The Charter Act.

Q. Who has been called the "Father of Education" in Tennessee?

A. Samuel Doak.

Q. When was Castle Heights Military Academy in Lebanon founded?

A. 1902.

Q. Who from Giles County became the United States Minister to Russia in 1850?

A. Neill S. Brown.

Q. Jean Faircloth of Murfreesboro, who was given numerous citations and medals following World War II for "outstanding and unselfish courage," was married to what man?

A. General Douglas MacArthur.

Q. What epidemic of 1849 was the cause of James K. Polk's death?

A. Cholera.

Q. Cave Johnson, born in Springfield in 1793, introduced what item into the United States postal system?

A. The postage stamp.

Q. What famous Cherokee chief led the attack on Fort Loudon in 1760?

A. Oconostota.

Q. On what ticket did John Bell, born in Davidson County, run for the United States presidency in 1860?

A. Constitutional Union ticket.

Q. Which member of the James Gang was captured at White's Creek on March 25, 1881?

A. William Ryan.

Q. Two Chattanooga men, B. F. Thomas and J. B. Whitehead, obtained the world's first "franchised bottling" of what drink?

A. Coca-Cola.

Q. Under President Grover Cleveland's administration, what Henry County-born personality served as United States Commissioner of Indian Affairs?

A. John DeWitt Clinton Atkins.

Q. Who was the first teacher in Middle Tennessee?

A. Ann Robertson Cockrill.

Q. What landmark was the first stone house in Knox County and the home of Knoxville's first elected mayor?

A. Ramsey House.

Q. Who was the wife of James Robertson, who saved Fort Nashborough by releasing dogs upon attacking Indians?

A. Charlotte Reeves Robertson.

Q. To what nation did France surrender all claims to land east of the Mississippi River?

A. England.

Q. What was the number of the engine in which Casey Jones was killed?

A. Old 382.

Q. Who was called the "poet-priest of our Confederacy" and served at Saint Michael's Mission in Robertson County in 1864-65?

A. Father Abram Ryan.

Q. Prentice Cooper was not only governor from 1939 to 1945 but later served as United States ambassador to what South American nation?

A. Peru.

Q. What Elizabethton native was the only person in American history to be both an admiral in the navy and a general in the army?

A. Samuel Powatan Carter.

Q. What was Nashville's first newspaper?

A. *Tennessee Gazette and Mero District Adviser,* 1787.

Q. What university first organized in 1834 in Murfreesboro was later relocated to Jackson?

A. Union University.

Q. What national award was given posthumously to Maury County native John Harlan Wills in 1945?

A. The Congressional Medal of Honor.

———◆———

Q. Who, following the Battle of Franklin on November 30, 1864, saw to the collecting and burying of the bodies of 1,496 Confederates?

A. John McGavock.

———◆———

Q. James C. Napier, prominent black Nashvillian, held what federal office?

A. Register of the United States Treasury, 1911-1915.

———◆———

Q. Who was called "the Pathfinder of the Sea" and was awarded more decorations by foreign governments for his discoveries and inventions than any other American?

A. Matthew Fontaine Maury.

———◆———

Q. Where was the first and only mint in Tennessee and the Southwest Territory?

A. Eaton's Station, about 9 miles southwest of Blountville.

———◆———

Q. What type of service was established from Nashville to Memphis and on to Little Rock, Arkansas in 1829?

A. Stagecoach.

———◆———

Q. What man was the first black president of the University of Tennessee at Martin, and was elected to an unprecedented second term?

A. Reginald Williams.

Q. What was the name of the first family to settle in Knoxville?

A. The James White family of North Carolina.

---◆---

Q. Who was the organizer and president of the Tennessee Central Railroad?

A. Jere Baxter.

---◆---

Q. What was the name of the early 1800s turnpike running across the Great Smokies between Macon County, North Carolina, and Blount County, Tennessee, that served as an important route in livestock commerce?

A. Tennessee River Turnpike.

---◆---

Q. Estes Kefauver, born in Madisonville, won recognition in 1950 as head of the United States Senate committee for investigating what subject?

A. Organized crime.

---◆---

Q. On September 21, 1906, what event in Jellico left nine dead, 200 injured, and 500 homeless?

A. A freight car loaded with more than ten tons of dynamite exploded.

---◆---

Q. Who in 1880 bequeathed $100,000 and property in downtown Nashville for the establishment of a free school for the poor?

A. Samuel Watkins.

---◆---

Q. Who was the well-to-do black Middle Tennessee landowner of the early 1800s who had over one hundred slaves?

A. Joe Clouston.

Q. What was the name of the first steamboat to navigate the Cumberland River to Nashville in March of 1819?

A. The *General Jackson.*

———◆———

Q. When did Tennessee secede from the union?

A. June 8, 1861.

———◆———

Q. George Gibbs Dibrell became president of which railroad in 1869?

A. The Southwestern Railroad.

———◆———

Q. During World War I, what Tennessean singlehandedly killed more than twenty Germans and forced a German major to surrender his entire group of 132 men?

A. Sergeant Alvin C. York.

———◆———

Q. While Tennessee was the last Confederate state to leave the union, where did it rank in returning?

A. First.

———◆———

Q. For what newspaper did Morgan C. Fitzpatrick, state representative, state Speaker of the House, state Superintendent of Schools, and congressman, serve as editor in the mid-1890's?

A. *Hartsville Vidette.*

———◆———

Q. Nashville lawyer James F. Neal served as prosecutor for the United States Department of Justice and won a conviction against which notable Teamsters Union leader?

A. Jimmy Hoffa, 1964.

Q. What museum now occupies the Lorraine Motel, where Martin Luther King, Jr., was assassinated?

A. The National Civil Rights Museum.

———◆———

Q. What was the name of the Cherokee Village from which the name Tennessee was derived?

A. Tanasi.

———◆———

Q. What event in 1779 led to the naming of Sale Creek in Hamilton County?

A. An auction of captured British supplies.

———◆———

Q. What Tennessean conceived the idea of the United Nations organization?

A. Cordell Hull.

———◆———

Q. Sarah Childress Polk prohibited what two things in the White House while she was first lady?

A. Dancing and drinking.

———◆———

Q. What Tennessean was in command of the USS *Nautilus* when it made the first submarine crossing of the North Pole in 1958?

A. William Anderson.

———◆———

Q. Who was the defender of the Alamo born in Sumner County in 1796 who was made famous by a knife that his brother, Reason, actually designed?

A. James Bowie.

Q. In 1966, Republicans won their first statewide office in Tennessee since 1920 by the election of what man?

A. Howard H. Baker, Jr., to the United States Senate.

Q. When was the first telegraph company chartered in the state?

A. 1847, New Orleans and Ohio Telegraph Company.

Q. What former slave who had helped clear the land for the first Maury County courthouse in 1808 put the first trowel of mortar on the cornerstone of the fourth courthouse in 1904?

A. Dick Porter.

Q. Serving as a nurse at the battlefields of Murfreesboro, Nashville, Pittsburg Landing and others, who was known as the "Florence Nightingale of America"?

A. Mary O'Connell.

Q. On August 17, 1967, the United States Postal Service issued a five cent commemorative stamp honoring what Tennessee hero?

A. Davy Crockett.

Q. What Lebanon native was the judge for the infamous Scopes trial?

A. Grafton Green.

Q. Young Confederate spy hero Sam Davis was hanged in what town?

A. Pulaski.

Q. What was the amount of the winning bid to construct the first state-funded road in 1804 from Kingston and Tellico to the Georgia line?

A. $1,499.95.

Q. What was the name of the racetrack in Unicoi County at which Andrew Jackson at age 21 rode his horse in a match race against a horse owned by Col. Robert Love and lost?

A. Greasy Cove Racetrack.

Q. In what city in 1941 did the Chicago and Southern Airline, the first airline to headquarter in the state, locate?

A. Memphis.

Q. How many days before governor Ray Blanton's term officially expired was governor-elect Lamar Alexander sworn in as governor of the state of Tennessee on January 17, 1979?

A. Three days.

Q. What Indians adopted teenager Sam Houston into their tribe?

A. The Cherokees.

Q. What group founded Maryville College in 1819?

A. The Synod of Tennessee, Presbyterian Church.

Q. What three United States presidents lived in Tennessee?

A. Andrew Jackson, James K. Polk and Andrew Johnson.

Q. Who was the Nashvillian who became the first American governor of California?

A. Peter Hardeman Burnett.

———◆———

Q. Nashville was made the permanent state capital on what date?

A. October 7, 1843.

———◆———

Q. Who was the Catholic priest, a native of North Nashville, made a cardinal in 1945 by Pope Pius XII?

A. Samuel Stritch.

———◆———

Q. What was the speed limit first imposed on Tennessee roads in 1905?

A. 20 mph.

———◆———

Q. William Banks Caperton, who was born in Spring Hill in 1855, held what high-ranking position with the Navy?

A. Commander-in-Chief of the Pacific Fleet, 1916.

———◆———

Q. What is the name of the oldest black-owned financial institution in the South, located in Nashville?

A. Citizen's Savings Bank.

———◆———

Q. What Middle Tennessee town was originally called Peters Camp Ground because of the numerous camp meetings held during its early settlement?

A. Spring Hill.

Q. What Chattanooga museum pays tribute to the winners of America's highest military award?

A. The Medal of Honor Museum.

Q. What name was given to the small pond at the Battle of Shiloh where the wounded of both armies came to seek water?

A. Bloody Pond.

Q. Who defeated his brother for the governorship in 1886?

A. Robert Love Taylor.

Q. Who was mayor of Knoxville at the time of the 1982 World's Fair?

A. Randy Tyree.

Q. Tennessee's Prohibition "bone-dry" laws were enacted in what year?

A. 1917.

Q. Why was Nashborough renamed Nashville?

A. Because of prejudice against the British-sounding "Nashborough."

Q. Who was the Blount County schoolteacher who went on to become governor of Tennessee, commander-in-chief of the Texas Army, president of the Republic of Texas, governor of Texas and United States senator from Texas?

A. Sam Houston.

Q. What former major-general of the Confederate Army and grandson of James Robertson had three horses shot from under him at the Battle of Stones River?

A. Benjamin Franklin Cheatham.

Q. In 1954 and again in 1979 what internationally known evangelist held meetings in Nashville?

A. Billy Graham.

Q. What was the amount of money given by Commodore Cornelius Vanderbilt in 1873 to establish Vanderbilt University?

A. One million dollars.

Q. Who designed the State Capitol building?

A. William Strickland.

Q. What editor of the *Nashville Tennessean* ran for governor in 1908?

A. Edward Ward Carmack.

Q. James "Lean Jimmy" Chamberlin Jones is noted for what first?

A. First native Tennessean to become governor.

Q. When was the first public high school organized in Chattanooga?

A. December, 1874.

Q. Which Pre-Columbian Indian culture found in Tennessee perfected the use of the bow and arrow?

A. Early Woodland Indians.

Q. Who established the first cotton gin and store in Brownsville?

A. Hiram Bradford.

Q. What special event took place on June 1, 1796?

A. Tennessee was admitted to the Union as a state.

Q. Who was the only-native born Tennessean to be knighted by the Crown of England?

A. Joseph Campbell (Sir Francis Joseph Campbell).

Q. Who were the contractors who rebuilt the Hermitage in 1835?

A. Joseph Rieff and William C. Hume.

Q. Who was the first governor to die in office?

A. Austin Peay.

Q. What congregation organized in 1827 in Franklin is called the "Mother Church of the Diocese of Tennessee"?

A. St. Paul's Episcopal Church.

Q. What Tennessee Democrat was the candidate for vice-president in 1956, running with presidential candidate Adlai E. Stevenson?

A. Estes Kefauver.

———◆———

Q. Who laid out the streets of the city of Knoxville in 1791?

A. Charles McClung.

———◆———

Q. What was the first bank in Tennessee?

A. The Nashville Bank, chartered in 1807 as a private bank and beginning business on March 1, 1810.

———◆———

Q. What member of Butch Cassidy's gang was in a shoot-out in Knoxville in December, 1901?

A. Harvey "Kid Curry" Logan.

———◆———

Q. Clinton Bowen Fisk, founder of Fisk University in Nashville, was a candidate for president of the United States in 1888 on what ticket?

A. Prohibitionist.

———◆———

Q. Where was the first wedding performed west of the Cumberland Mountains?

A. Fort Nashborough, the marriage of Capt. James Lieper and Susan Drake.

———◆———

Q. What famous frontiersman served Tennessee in Congress from 1827 to 1831 and from 1833 to 1835?

A. Davy Crockett.

Q. Who was Andrew Jackson's wife?

A. Rachel Donelson Jackson, whose father helped found Nashville.

Q. Who was the last settler killed by Indians in Knox County?

A. George Mann.

Q. In what county was Sam Houston's boyhood home?

A. Blount County.

Q. Who was the youngest lawyer ever to practice in the state of Tennessee, being admitted to the bar at age 18?

A. Beverly Briley, who was judge and Mayor of Nashville for many years.

Q. What is the oldest remaining covered bridge in Tennessee?

A. The Doe River bridge in Elizabethton.

Q. In what year was the Tennessee–Tombigbee Waterway first proposed?

A. 1874.

Q. What Confederate brigadier-general was nicknamed "Wizard of the Saddle" due to his hit-and-run cavalry tactics?

A. Nathan Bedford Forrest.

Q. Which two early explorers explored the western part of Tennessee for France?

A. Louis Joliet and Jaques Marquette, 1673.

Q. What were the call letters of the first radio station in the state, owned and operated in Lawrenceburg by James D. Vaughan?

A. WOAN.

Q. The introduction of what mechanical device into the Pre-Columbian Archaic Indians of Tennessee greatly improved the use of the hunting spear?

A. The atlatl, or spear thrower.

Q. What presidential candidate was elected as the first "dark horse" president?

A. James K. Polk.

Q. What was the first public school in Nashville, opened in 1855?

A. Fogg (now Hume-Fogg).

Q. During whose governorship were the laws allowing women to vote and workman's compensation passed?

A. Albert H. Roberts, 1919-1921.

Q. Staff sergeant Raymond H. Cooley of Dunlap received what high decoration for his performance during the invasion of the Philippines in 1945?

A. The Congressional Medal of Honor.

Q. Who was the first permanent white settler in Tennessee who in 1779, in Washington County, built a cabin on a site previously used by Daniel Boone as a hunting camp?

A. William Bean.

◆

Q. Who was the Tennessee Supreme Court judge who died from being impaled on a broken piece of his walking cane during a fall?

A. William Bruce Turley.

◆

Q. What was the name of the gunboat, under the command of Tennessean Washburn Maynard, that fired the first shot of the Spanish-American War?

A. The *Nashville*.

◆

Q. Who mustered a company of 57 volunteers in Hamblen County for the War with Mexico?

A. Captain William Atkinson.

◆

Q. In 1919, what Franklin native was part of an unofficial mission to kidnap Kaiser Wilhelm?

A. Thomas P. Henderson.

◆

Q. Who from Memphis was chosen "Miss America" in 1947?

A. Barbara Jo Walker.

◆

Q. Who was the famous ironmaster who directed the tunneling through the cliffs at the "Narrows of the Harpeth" to operate forge equipment?

A. Montgomery Bell.

Q. Under whose governorship was the first hospital for the mentally ill established in the state?

A. William Carroll.

Q. For what man is Nashville named?

A. General Francis Nash, a Revolutionary War hero.

Q. Alexandria was the original name of what West Tennessee city?

A. Jackson.

Q. For what "first" was King Ironworks in Sullivan County noted?

A. The first nail factory in the state.

Q. Jesse Bean, the first permanent settler in Franklin County, became famous for producing what product?

A. 45-inch long rifles.

Q. In what year was gold discovered along Coker Creek in Monroe County?

A. 1831.

Q. What little Indian boy, orphaned during the Creek War, was taken in by Andrew Jackson and raised as his own son?

A. Lincoya.

Q. What disease was responsible for one of the worst epidemics in United States history that hit Memphis in 1878?

A. Yellow fever.

———◆———

Q. What Tennessean was named the first full admiral in the United States Navy in 1866?

A. David Glasgow Farragut.

———◆———

Q. On what Nashville street was the first Governor's Mansion?

A. North Vine (now North Seventh).

———◆———

Q. Who was the character of southern folklore said to have sent Andrew Jackson retreating from Robertson County back to Nashville?

A. The Bell Witch.

———◆———

Q. What was the total paid attendance of the 1897 Centennial Exposition?

A. 1,273,827.

———◆———

Q. How did Tennessee rank chronologically in joining the Union?

A. Sixteenth.

———◆———

Q. Who was the carpetbagger mayor of Nashville who plundered the public with his corrupt administration until being run out of town under judicial pressure?

A. A. E. Alden.

Q. Who was the Sumner County-born unsuccessful candidate for the vice-presidency of the United States on the Know-Nothing ticket in 1856?

A. Andrew Jackson Donelson.

Q. Who officially opened the Centennial Exposition on May 1, 1897 by pressing a button in Washinton that fired a gun in Centennial Park in Nashville?

A. President McKinley.

Q. The twenty-dollar bill bears the portrait of which notable Tennessean?

A. Andrew Jackson.

Q. How many men did the Army of Tennessee lose in the five-hour Battle of Franklin in 1864?

A. 6,202.

Q. Rocky Mount near Johnson City was built in 1770 for what purpose?

A. Territorial capital.

Q. What was the name of the vigilante group, organized in Sevierville in 1892 and disbanded in 1898, that styled itself after the Ku Klux Klan.

A. The White Caps.

Q. What was the name of the automobile produced by Southern Motor Works in Nashville prior to World War I?

A. Marathon.

Q. Who was the powerful boss of the Memphis political machine elected mayor of that city in 1909?

A. E. H. Crump.

Q. The first Catholic Church in Tennessee was built in 1820 in what city?

A. Nashville.

Q. Who held a record six terms as governor?

A. William Carroll.

Q. Who was the Nashvillian who appointed himself in 1853 to be president of Lower California and was elected president of Nicaragua in 1856?

A. William Walker.

Q. Which United States president's father was an early professor of theology at Southwestern Presbyterian University, which was originally located in Clarksville and later relocated in Memphis?

A. Woodrow Wilson.

Q. What East Tennessee home was the first capitol of the "Territory South of the River Ohio"?

A. Rocky Mount, the Cobb-Massengill Home.

Q. Tennessee has favored which political party for most of its history?

A. The Democratic Party.

Q. Who raised the flag of the United States for the first time over former Spanish possessions in 1797, proclaiming exclusive sovereignty of the United States on the Mississippi River?

A. Capt. Isaac Guion.

Q. Under what name was the institution that eventually became the University of Tennessee first chartered?

A. Blount College, Knoxville.

Q. Who is called the "Father of Tennessee"?

A. James Robertson.

Q. What was the real name of "Casey" Jones, the railroad man, who received his nickname from spending time in Cayce, Kentucky?

A. John Luther Jones.

Q. What Indian tribe ceded their claims to Tennessee to the English in 1768?

A. Iroquois.

Q. Who was made the first Grand Wizard and chief officer of the Ku Klux Klan?

A. General Nathan Bedford Forrest.

Q. Who was awarded the contract to construct the first state-funded road in Tennessee?

A. Adam Peck.

Q. Near what present-day city did Juan Pedro and a group of Spaniards establish a fort in 1566?

A. Chattanooga.

Q. What was the name of the "real life" person known as the Bell Witch?

A. Kate Batts.

Q. What astronaut couple were married May 30, 1981, in Murfreesboro?

A. Dr. Rhea Seddon and Robert "Hoot" Gibson.

Q. Who was the Confederate soldier, journalist, and political leader who spent most of his boyhood in Coffee County and founded the *Louisville Courier-Journal* in 1868?

A. Henry Watterson.

Q. What man could be called "The Forgotten Founder" of Nashville?

A. Judge Richard Henderson, who wrote the Cumberland Compact and financed and directed the overland and river expeditions.

Q. For whom was Knoxville named?

A. General Henry Knox (1750-1806), United States secretary of war. Knox was William Blount's immediate superior over Indian matters, and Blount was the one who named Knoxville.

Q. Sam Houston was adopted by the Cherokees and given what name?

A. The Raven.

ARTS & LITERATURE

C H A P T E R   F O U R

Q. Nashville-born primitive sculptor William Edmondson was the first black artist to have a one-man show at what internationally famous art museum?

A. New York Museum of Modern Art.

———◆———

Q. What theatrical organization was formed in 1818 with Sam Houston as its secretary and Andrew Jackson as an honorary member?

A. Thespian Society of Nashville.

———◆———

Q. Knoxville-born James Agee wrote the screenplay for what Humphrey Bogart, Katherine Hepburn movie classic?

A. *African Queen.*

———◆———

Q. Beth Slater Whitson of Centerville wrote what hit song in 1912?

A. *Let Me Call You Sweetheart.*

———◆———

Q. Which country comedian is a noted watercolor painter?

A. Archie Campbell.

Q. Who was the famous playwright who lived in Nashville for two years around 1916 and took the name "Tennessee" in 1939?

A. Thomas Lanier "Tennessee" Williams.

———◆———

Q. What was the name of the first newspaper published in the state?

A. *The Knoxville Gazette.*

———◆———

Q. Who founded the Nashville Symphony?

A. Dr. George Pullen Jackson, in 1920.

———◆———

Q. What Nashvillian is the author of *Murphy's Fault,* chosen by the *New York Times* as one of 1989's best mystery novels?

A. Steven Womack.

———◆———

Q. Who was the Peabody College graduate from Ripley who authored *The Preacher's Son* and was named poet laureate of Georgia in 1943?

A. Wrightman Fletcher Melton.

———◆———

Q. What 1917 classic of the great outdoors was re-published by the University of Tennessee Press in 1988?

A. Horace Kephart's *Camping and Woodcraft.*

———◆———

Q. One of the nation's largest book manufacturers is located in which northeastern Tennessee community?

A. Kingsport, Kingsport Press.

Q. What architect is buried in a vault in the north wall of the state capitol building?

A. William Strickland, its builder.

Q. What songwriting couple wrote such great hits as *All I Have To Do Is Dream, Bird Dog, Bye, Bye Love,* and *Rocky Top*?

A. Felice and Boudleaux Bryant, Hendersonville.

Q. What is the name of the book binding process utilizing glued pages instead of sewn pages that was developed at Kingsport Press?

A. Perfect binding.

Q. What Memphis girl grew to fame as an artist by painting the first portrait ever done of Hsiao-ch'in, Dowager Empress of China?

A. Katherine Augusta Carl, known as Kate.

Q. What was the title of the first poem composed in Tennessee territory and published in a newspaper in Lexington, Kentucky in 1799?

A. *Account of Remarkable Occurrences* by Col. James Smith.

Q. Who was the Scottish playwright who established a colony for emancipated slaves in Tennessee called Nashoba?

A. Francis "Fanny" Wright.

Q. Born in the town of Tuskegee in Monroe County in 1760, Sequoyah is most noted for what accomplishment?

A. He designed an 85-character alphabet still in use in the Cherokee Nation.

Q. *A Cry of Absence* is the civil rights novel of what Vanderbilt alumnus?

A. Madison Jones.

Q. What are the four state songs of Tennessee?

A. *The Tennessee Waltz, When It's Iris Time in Tennessee, My Tennessee,* and *Rocky Top.*

Q. In 1823 on Sulphur Creek in Hickman County craftsman Adain Coble established what type of manufacturing firm?

A. Pottery.

Q. Who is the author of the famous *Tom Brown's School Days*?

A. Thomas Hughes, who also founded the English colony of Rugby in Moran and Scott counties.

Q. In which area of textile art are Jan Broderson of Overton county, Betsy Worden of Knoxville and Judy Elwood of Oak Ridge well known?

A. Wall-hanging sculpture.

Q. Will T. Hale of Clarksville is noted for verse and prose works such as *Showers and Sunshine,* (1896), and *The Backward Trail,* (1899), but was also editor of which three Tennessee newspapers?

A. Memphis *Commercial Appeal,* Nashville *American,* and Knoxville *Sentinel.*

Q. Of the sixteen members of the Fugitives, what four were the most influential?

A. Allen Tate, John Crowe Ransom, Donald Davidson, Robert Penn Warren.

Q. Where was "Blind Joe" Mangum, the concert radio violinist and musical genius widely known for his arrangement and performances of Septimus Winner's song *Listen To The Mockingbird* born?

A. Dresden.

Q. What Nashvillian authored the book *Sky Diving*?

A. Bud Sellick.

Q. What was the architectural style that swept through the state from the 1830s until the War Between the States?

A. Greek Revival.

Q. Established by Elihu Embree at Jonesboro, what was the first journal published in the United States completely devoted to the anti-slavery movement?

A. *Manumission Intelligencer.*

Q. Rattle and Snap, the mansion home of George Polk, is considered to be one of the nation's finest examples of what type architecture?

A. Greek Revival.

Q. In what year was Brooks Memorial Art League, the first systematized art library in the state, established in Memphis?

A. 1936.

Q. Who founded the Newport newspaper, *Plain Talk,* and served in both the Tennessee and United States House of Representatives?

A. William Coleman Anderson.

Q. What was the method of reading music that was popular in Tennessee through the first half of the 20th century, that had its origins in England during the time of Shakespeare?

A. Shaped notes.

Q. Who was the painter who lived as a part of Andrew Jackson's household for close to twenty years?

A. Ralph E. W. Earl.

Q. What Knoxville-born, Fisk University-educated poet has twelve published volumes and has won acclaim by capturing the pure essence of special family relationships?

A. Nikki Giovanni.

Q. What country music songwriter is the author of the novel *Spring Hill*?

A. Tom T. Hall.

Q. What artist painted the large wall murals depicting the history of Nashville in the Opryland Hotel?

A. T. Max Hochstettler.

Q. Mrs. W. H. McCarter of Gatlinburg is noted for what handwoven textile pattern?

A. *Tennessee Blazing Star.*

Q. What religious group was very vocal during the 1820s and 30s concerning their opposition to attending theatrical productions?

A. The Methodists.

Q. What two murals in the State Office Building in Nashville depict the discovery of the territory and the development of the state of Tennessee?

A. The Cornwall Murals.

———◆———

Q. *The Store*, a 1933 Pulitzer Prize winning novel, is the second in a trilogy including *The Forge* (1931) and *Unfinished Cathedral* (1934) written by which Clifton author?

A. T. S. Stribling

———◆———

Q. What Memphian is the author of *The Tennessee Truckers Roundup*?

A. John L. LeMay.

———◆———

Q. What turn of the century Knoxville photographer pioneered the style of staged folk narrative in his work and the use of soft focus for portraits?

A. Joseph Knaffl.

———◆———

Q. What is APTA, which has nineteen chapters and operates eleven historic sites?

A. The Association for Preservation of the Tennessee Antiquities.

———◆———

Q. Who was the author of *Trigonometry, Plane and Spherical* and was the first chancellor of Vanderbilt University?

A. Landon Cabell Garland.

———◆———

Q. What Nashville nutritionist co-authored the best-selling *The T-Factor Fat Gram Counter* with Dr. Martin Katahn?

A. Jamie Pope-Cordle.

Q. What is the name of the school founded in 1925 as a free center of instruction for the arts in Memphis?

A. James Lee Memorial Academy of Arts.

———◆———

Q. What Tennessee resident is well known for her creation of the McKinnon family of Mattagash, Maine?

A. Cathie Pelletier.

———◆———

Q. What Nashvillian has authored many children's books, including *Six Patches and the Dragon*, and is also a master puppeteer?

A. Tom Tichenor.

———◆———

Q. What Nashvillian is the most noted female gospel music composer of this century?

A. Dottie Rambo.

———◆———

Q. Painter George DeForest Brush, born in Shelbyville in 1885, is noted for what subject matters?

A. Indian life and group portraits.

———◆———

Q. What Tennessee literary quarterly is the oldest in the nation?

A. *The Sewanee Review.*

———◆———

Q. Various women's groups interested in developing musical appreciation in Tennessee merged in 1916 to form what organization?

A. Tennessee Federation of Music Clubs.

Q. Who was the noted Nashville black poet and scholar who produced the great work *God's Trombones* (1927), which was comprised of seven black sermons in verse?

A. James Weldon Johnson.

———◆———

Q. When did the first recorded theatrical performance take place in Nashville?

A. December 4, 1807.

———◆———

Q. What was the name of the newspaper published for several months from a boxcar that traveled with Confederate armies during the War Between the States?

A. *Chattanooga Daily Rebel.*

———◆———

Q. What great country writer wrote *Pick Me up on Your Way Down, Second Hand Rose, I Fall to Pieces* (co-written with Hank Cochran), *Heartaches by the Number, I've Got a Tiger by the Tail, Heartbreak U.S.A.*, and more?

A. Harlan Howard.

———◆———

Q. When did the Federal Government set up its first federally funded art project in Tennessee?

A. December, 1933.

———◆———

Q. The serious verse *Songs of East and West* (1906) and *Hernando DeSoto* (1914), a lengthy narrative in verse, were the works of what Memphian?

A. Walter Malone.

———◆———

Q. Architect Edward Dougherty won a national award for his design of what building?

A. The War Memorial Building in Nashville, built in 1925.

Q. Who was the internationally-known author of children's books, born in Franklin, whose award-winning books included *Flaming Arrows*, *The Buffalo Knife* and *The Old Wilderness Road*?

A. William Owen Steele.

---◆---

Q. Who was the syndicated advice columnist born in Montgomery County?

A. Elizabeth Meriwether 'Dorothy Dix' Gilmer.

---◆---

Q. What book did sports editor Fred Russell author on Vanderbilt football?

A. *Fifty Years of Vanderbilt Football*.

---◆---

Q. Who was the outstanding New York advertising executive and author of the 1924 best seller *The Man Nobody Knows* who was born in Robbins?

A. Bruce Barton.

---◆---

Q. What outstanding writer of the Local Color Movement lived in Murfreesboro and wrote about the mountains of East Tennessee?

A. Mary Noailles Murfree.

---◆---

Q. What special event was held at the Kennedy Center on August 7, 1977?

A. It was Memphis Night in the nation's capital, with three Metropolitan Opera singers who grew up in Memphis performing: Ruth Welting, Nancy Tatum and Mignon Dunn.

---◆---

Q. What artist painted Chattanooga's most famous painting of Colonel James A. Whitesides and his family at Umbrella Rock on Lookout Mountain?

A. James Cameron.

Q. Who was the gospel music composer, whose first hymn book sold millions of copies and who founded a music publishing company in Chattanooga in 1929 that later was relocated to Dayton?

A. Robert E. Winsett.

———◆———

Q. Terry Weeks, 1988 National Teacher of the Year, now teaches at what institution?

A. Middle Tennessee State University.

———◆———

Q. Hancock county is one of the last locations in the nation for the practice of what craft?

A. Cooperage, the construction of buckets, churns, tubs, and so forth, from wooden slats often without the use of nails or glue.

———◆———

Q. Yolande Cornelia Giovanni, one of the most significant Tennessee black poets of the latter half of the twentieth century, was born in which city?

A. Knoxville.

———◆———

Q. Margaret Anderson wrote what moving and inspirational book on the troubles of her Tennessee and the South?

A. *The Children of the South*.

———◆———

Q. What opera based on a famous Tennessee love story premiered in Knoxville in April 1989?

A. *Rachel*.

———◆———

Q. What Vanderbilt professor of English wrote *An Outland Piper, Lee in the Mountains* and *The Tennessee River*?

A. Donald Grady Davidson.

Q. What 1975 Lisa Alther novel follows Ginny Hull as she grows up in Hullsport, Tennessee?

A. *Kinflicks.*

———◆———

Q. John Haywood is noted for what two outstanding works on Tennessee?

A. *The Civil and Political History of Tennessee* and *Aboriginal History of Tennessee.*

———◆———

Q. Which Memphis-born composer wrote the popular hit *The Yellow Rose of Texas*?

A. Bob Miller.

———◆———

Q. What is the name of one of O. Henry's (William Sydney Porter) best short stories, which originated from a visit he made to his daughter who was attending Ward-Belmont finishing school in Nashville?

A. *A Municipal Report.*

———◆———

Q. The first full-sized model of the Parthenon was constructed of wood and plaster at the 1897 Centennial Exposition and used for what purpose?

A. To house the Municipal Art Gallery.

———◆———

Q. What Knox County Sheriff's Department officer is the author of *The Moon Is Always Full*, *Black Friday Coming Down*, and *The Jigsaw Man*?

A. David Hunter.

———◆———

Q. What university produces proportionally more Rhodes scholars than any other school in the nation?

A. The University of the South.

Q. What Nashville songwriter became famous for his songs: *A Little Bitty Tear, Don't Touch Me, I Want to Go with You, Make the World Go Away, She's Got You,* and *I Fall to Pieces* (co-written with Harlan Howard)?

A. Hank Cochran.

———◆———

Q. What author moved from New York to Chattanooga and has entertained scores of young twentieth century readers with tales of Tennessee history?

A. Christine Noble Govan.

———◆———

Q. What early usher at the Staub's Theatre in Knoxville later became publisher of the *New York Times*?

A. Adolph Ochs.

———◆———

Q. What composer, concert and radio organist, born in Franklin, was decorated by King Albert of Belgium in 1932 for distinguished musical services?

A. Alexander Russell.

———◆———

Q. The design of the 290-foot tall arena in Memphis is based on what historical landmark?

A. The Great Pyramid of Cheops.

———◆———

Q. What native Nashvillian is nationally known for her sculpting and has works in Nashville, Chattanooga, New York City, Washington, D.C. and Annapolis?

A. Belle Kinney Scholz.

———◆———

Q. What Nashville firm is the largest commercial Bible publisher in the world?

A. Thomas Nelson Publishers, Nashville.

Q. What was the name of Mark Twain's work dealing with fist fights, duels and horse whippings among newspaper editors?

A. *Journalism in Tennessee.*

———◆———

Q. What Vanderbilt alumnus is best known for his works *Understanding Poetry* and *Understanding Fiction?*

A. Cleanth Brooks.

———◆———

Q. Poet Randall Jarrell was born in Nashville in 1914 and is best known for which one of his works?

A. *Death of the Ball Turrett Gunner.*

———◆———

Q. How many people attended the first Southern Festival of Books in 1989?

A. 25,000.

———◆———

Q. *The Sequel of Appomattox,* (1921) is a study of the Reconstruction days written by what Nashvillian?

A. Walter L. Fleming.

———◆———

Q. Who was the University of Tennessee at Knoxville graduate whose novel *The Day of the Minotaur,* won a "Hugo" science fiction award nomination in 1966?

A. Thomas Burnett Swann.

———◆———

Q. Will Allen Dromgoole, author of *The Heart of Old Hickory, Harum Scarum Joe* and *Fortunes of the Fellow* was the literary editor for what newspaper?

A. *Nashville Daily Banner.*

Q. What newspaper was moved several times through the South during the War Between the States in an attempt to keep the journalistic flag of the Confederacy flying?

A. *The Memphis Daily Appeal.*

◆

Q. Who was designated Tennessee's official Poet Laureate for life on May 28, 1977 by House Joint Resolution No. 250 of the 90th General Assembly?

A. Richard M. "Pek" Gunn.

◆

Q. Who was the Nashvillian who served as expedition artist for the Peary North Greenland Expeditions in 1892 and 1892-93?

A. Frank Wilbert Stokes.

◆

Q. Actress/model Cybill Shepherd of Memphis gained what title in 1968?

A. Model of the Year.

◆

Q. Who was the sculptor responsible for creating the equestrian statue of Andrew Jackson on the state capitol grounds?

A. Clark Miller.

◆

Q. The State Library was founded in what year?

A. 1853.

◆

Q. What Memphis poet and attorney published two volumes of poetry before he was twenty?

A. Walter Malone.

Q. Who is the Nashville advertising and public relations executive who is internationally known for his paintings and prints?

A. Paul Harmon.

———◆———

Q. Who first brought symphony music to Tennessee?

A. Theodore Thomas in the 1870s.

———◆———

Q. Mildred Haun of Hamblen County wrote what novel depicting the life of Tennessee women in very cruel and stoic terms?

A. *The Hawk's Done Gone.*

———◆———

Q. Who was the Nashvillian who in 1902 founded a gospel music publishing company that grew into a giant in the gospel music publishing and recording industry?

A. John T. Benson, Benson Publishing.

———◆———

Q. Mary Noailles Murfree of Murfreesboro, who wrote for the *Atlantic Monthly* in the late 1800s and had 25 novels to her credit, chose to write under what man's pseudonym?

A. Charles Egbert Craddock.

———◆———

Q. Poets who during the late 1920s and early 30s expressed the Southern lifestyle versus the lifestyles of the rest of the nation were known by what title?

A. The Tennessee Agrarians.

———◆———

Q. What was the name of the Knoxville photographer whose first love was painting scenes of the Great Smokies?

A. Charles Christopher Krutch.

Q. What institution was established in 1855 in Nashville for the advancement of the arts?

A. Nashville Academy of Music and Fine Arts.

◆

Q. What Knox County novelist won the William Faulkner Foundation Award and the Travel Award of the American Academy of Arts and Letters for his first novel *The Orchard Keeper* (1965)?

A. Cormac McCarthy.

◆

Q. What Columbia landmark built in 1835 is distinguished by its Moorish design of the Gothic period?

A. The Athenaeum.

◆

Q. What MTSU professor is the author of *Tennessee Strings* and *Kentucky Country*?

A. Charles Wolfe.

◆

Q. Who was known as the "man of a thousand portraits"?

A. Washington Cooper.

◆

Q. What instrument of three or four strings had great popularity among the mountain folk of East Tennessee and was often handmade by local craftsmen?

A. The Appalachian Mountain dulcimer.

◆

Q. Lanie Dill, an executive of the 3M Company in Nashville, compiled, wrote, edited and published what book that was on the paperback bestseller list for nine weeks in 1976?

A. *The "Official" CB Slanguage Language Dictionary.*

Q. Homer A. Rodeheaver, noted sacred publisher, singer and trombonist who traveled with evangelist Billy Sunday, worked as a youth in his father's mill in what community?

A. Jellico.

———◆———

Q. What is the name of the interesting study of medieval medicines and the role they played in Chaucer's *Canterbury Tales* written in 1926 by Vanderbilt professor Dr. Walter Clyde Curry?

A. *Chaucer and the Medieval Sciences.*

———◆———

Q. What international film festival is held in Nashville each summer?

A. Sinking Creek.

———◆———

Q. What Tennessee native and author of *Shrovetide in Old New Orleans* published a collection of poetry entitled *Chattanooga*?

A. Ishmael Reed.

———◆———

Q. Who authored the book *Portraits in Tennessee Painted Before 1866*?

A. Eleanor Morrissey.

———◆———

Q. In what historic Knoxville neighborhood have turn-of-the-century homes been turned into a miniature artists' colony?

A. Fort Sanders.

———◆———

Q. Who was the colorful Tennessee newspaperman shot to death in 1908 by a disgruntled reader?

A. Edward Ward Carmack.

Q. Thomas Hart Benton, grandnephew and namesake of the man who dueled Andrew Jackson on the public square in Nashville, painted the mural entitled *The Sources of Country Music* for what museum?

A. The Country Music Hall of Fame and Museum in Nashville, 1974.

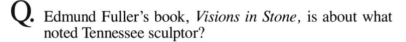

Q. What Nashville attorney is the author of *Triple Jeopardy* and *Desperate Justice*?

A. Richard Speight.

Q. Edmund Fuller's book, *Visions in Stone,* is about what noted Tennessee sculptor?

A. William Edmondson.

Q. Each summer the drama, *Walk Toward the Sunset,* is performed in what county?

A. Hancock County.

Q. What is the name of America's oldest Bible publisher, now headquartered in Nashville?

A. Holman Bible Publishers.

Q. What award did Alex Haley receive for his book *Roots*?

A. A special Pulitzer Prize.

Q. What was the title of James Adair's book, the first book written west of the Appalachians and published in 1775?

A. *History of the American Indians.*

Q. *The Railroad Advocate*, the first paper in the United States devoted exclusively to railroad promotion, started publication in 1831 in what town?

A. Rogersville.

———◆———

Q. For what type of writing was Alfred Leland Crabbe of Peabody College in Nashville noted?

A. Historical novels.

———◆———

Q. What film made in Tennessee was based on Madison Jones's novel, *The Exile*?

A. *I Walk the Line*.

———◆———

Q. What artist couple created a large ceramic stoneware mural (10 feet by 40 feet) for the Cumberland Museum and Science Center depicting the ecological and geological features of Davidson County?

A. Ronald and Judi Lederer, Nashville.

———◆———

Q. The *Problem of Stuttering* was written by what psychologist born in Rutherford County?

A. John Madison Fletcher.

———◆———

Q. Who was the great painter who settled in Knoxville around 1880 and was capable of elevating everyday, common scenes to sublime dimensions?

A. Lloyd Branson.

———◆———

Q. In what town was Pulitzer Prize-winning author, Thomas Sigismund 'T.S.' Stribling born?

A. Clifton.

Q. Who was the author of *Dramatic Life as I Found It* who also organized a drama club in Nashville in 1818?

A. Noah Miller Ludlow.

———◆———

Q. Who were the sculptors who faithfully reproduced the sculpture work on the Parthenon in Nashville?

A. George J. Zolnay, Belle Kenney and Leopold Scholz.

———◆———

Q. What author wrote *Come Next Spring*, a young adult novel set in Tennessee in the 1940s?

A. Alana White.

———◆———

Q. In 1990, what two Tennessee newspapers ended the joint operating agreement that had been in operation since 1957?

A. *Knoxville News-Sentinel* and *Knoxville Journal*.

———◆———

Q. What publication was considered the Agrarian Manifesto?

A. *I'll Take My Stand*.

———◆———

Q. What author wrote about her hometown of Clarksville in 1937, telling of its fascination and frustrations?

A. Evelyn Scott, *Background in Tennessee*.

———◆———

Q. Who was the United States commissioner of education from 1911-1921 and author of *Effective English* who was born in Bedford County?

A. Philander Priestley Claxton.

Q. Who is the award-winning historical writer who lives in Franklin, has authored numerous works and is editor of *Your Tennessee*, which is used in all Tennessee public schools?

A. James A. Crutchfield.

Q. What famous artist from Morgan County painted a portrait of Mrs. James K. Polk that hangs today in the East Room of the White House?

A. George Dury.

Q. Mrs. E. L. Ashford of Nashville compiled a music book entitled *Organ Instructions*, which was the first book of its type to be translated into what language?

A. Chinese.

Q. What noted Civil War historian is also the author of *Love in a Dry Season* and *Tournament*?

A. Shelby Foote.

Q. Who was the librarian at Fisk University from 1943 to 1965 who authored *Story of the Negro* and *Story of George Washington Carver*?

A. Arna Wendell Bontemps.

Q. Virginia Frazer Boyle, born near Chattanooga and author of *The Other Side* and *Christ in the Argonne*, received what special office in 1910 created by the United Confederate Veterans?

A. Poet Laureate.

Q. What native Nashvillian was a poet, philanthropist and financier and was considered for a Nobel Peace Prize for the development of Youth Incorporated and the 'Hands Across the Sea' project of 1950?

A. Allen Dobsen.

Q. Who was the eminent author who lived in Knoxville whose most famous work was *Little Lord Fauntleroy,* a parody of her son who was born in Knoxville?

A. Frances Hodgson Burnett.

———◆———

Q. What is the name of the large gospel music publisher with a branch office in Chattanooga that did so much toward creating a musical style known throughout the southeast as convention music?

A. Stamps-Baxter Music.

———◆———

Q. In three years of publication, how many issues of *The Fugitive* were released?

A. Nineteen.

———◆———

Q. Who founded the *Knoxville Post* in 1841?

A. James Williams.

———◆———

Q. What Nashvillian is the author of many children's books as well as *Fullness of Time?*

A. Martha Whitmore Hickman.

———◆———

Q. What was the purpose in the formation of the Old Harp Singers in 1932 by Dr. George Pullen Jackson of Vanderbilt?

A. To preserve traditional folk music.

———◆———

Q. Who was the first president of the Tennessee Woman's Press Club and author of *Sunny Bunny Rabbit and His Friends?*

A. Grace McGowan Cooke.

Q. What naturalist wrote about his hiking the Appalachian Trail in *As Far As the Eye Can See*?

A. David Brill.

Q. What noted nineteenth century American lithographers captured Nashville's favorite filly, Peytona, beating the New York horse, Fashion, at the running of the Long Island "race of the century" in 1845?

A. Currier and Ives.

Q. What is the name of the well-known black artist who painted the wall murals of the Fisk University library in the 1930s?

A. Aaron K. Douglass.

Q. Lycrecia Williams wrote what biography of her mother and stepfather, Audrey and Hank Williams?

A. *Still in Love with You.*

Q. What lady who lived near Madison wrote such titles as *Rose of Old Harpeth, Over Paradise Ridge, The Road to Providence, Equal Franchise,* and *The Elected Mother*?

A. Maria Thompson Daviess.

Q. Where is an exact, full-size replica of the Parthenon in Athens to be found?

A. Centennial Park, Nashville.

Q. What Knoxvillian was awarded the Pulitzer Prize for *A Death In the Family*?

A. James Agee.

Q. What former reporter for the *Nashville Tennessean* (1956–60) won a Pulitzer prize for international reporting?

A. David Halberstam.

Q. In 1922 a group of poets was organized at Vanderbilt University to express their self-convicted experimentalist poems and became known by what title?

A. The Fugitive Group.

Q. Where is the Hunter Museum of Art situated?

A. Chattanooga.

Q. Who is the noted knife maker from Cleveland who specializes in historical knives such as the Bowie knife and the Arkansas Toothpick?

A. Harold Crisp.

Q. Bertha Walbun Clark was the first director of what symphony that grew from an orchestral ensemble she organized in 1910?

A. Knoxville Symphony Orchestra.

Q. Who was the first novelist in the state?

A. Charles Todd, a Presbyterian minister, with his work *Woodville, or The Anchored Return,* 1832.

Q. Who was the novelist born in Nashville who wrote *A Tennessee Judge, An American in New York,* and *In the Alamo*?

A. Charles Ready.

Q. Melchior Thoni, a woodcarver and cabinet maker from Switzerland, moved to Nashville in 1869 and designed and carved the first wooden animals to stand upon what apparatus?

A. A "Flying Jenny" (a merry-go-round).

◆

Q. Who was the 1979 National Book Award winner, author and recognized authority on early American literature?

A. Richard Beale Davis.

◆

Q. Which book by John Haywood, published in 1834, gave great insight into the mixing of civilization and frontier conditions?

A. *The Life of David Crockett of Tennessee.*

◆

Q. Cheekwood, the former residence of the founder of the Maxwell House Coffee empire, is presently used for what?

A. Tennessee Botanical Gardens and Fine Arts Center, Nashville.

◆

Q. Henri Christian Weber, a German-born composer who settled in Nashville in the 1850s, composed what song used at the nation's centennial celebration at Philadelphia in 1876?

A. *The Centennial March.*

◆

Q. What author of *Ain't Nothin' Sweet As My Baby* claims to be the daughter of country star Hank Williams?

A. Jett Williams.

◆

Q. What authors of *The Quilts of Tennessee* were responsible for a museum exhibit of the same name?

A. Merikay Waldvogel and Bets Ramsey.

Q. Country music composer Dallas Frazier of Madison wrote what song that went to number one in the pop field and sold over a million copies?

A. *Alley Oop.*

Q. For what collection of essays dealing with black history, published in 1903, was Fisk university student W. E. B. DuBois noted?

A. *The Souls of Black Folk.*

Q. Which Tennessee watercolor painter is known for her minutely-textured works showing dilapidated barns sitting in uncultivated fields?

A. Pauline Wallen.

Q. What art collection was brought from Japan to be exhibited in Nashville in 1990–91?

A. The Bridgestone Collection.

Q. Who was the author from Lauderdale County from whose stories the play *The Green Pastures* was adapted?

A. Roark Bradford.

Q. Who is the author of the award-winning novel *A Summons to Memphis*?

A. Peter Taylor.

Q. *Tennessee Off the Beaten Path* is the work of what author?

A. Tim O'Brien.

Q. Who was the Chattanooga blues singer who contributed significantly to the development of jazz in the 1920's?

A. Elizabeth "Bessie" Smith.

———◆———

Q. What Nashvillian wrote *The Americanization of Dixie*?

A. John Egerton.

———◆———

Q. What organization was formed in 1979 to help encourage filmmaking in Tennessee?

A. The Tennessee Film Commission.

———◆———

Q. Who is the noted political cartoonist who has worked for both Nashville and Memphis newspapers and produced his own syndicated comic strip called *The Ryatts*?

A. Calvin "Cal" Lane Alley.

———◆———

Q. What are the two largest publishers of religious materials in the state?

A. The Baptist Sunday School Board and The United Methodist Publishing House.

———◆———

Q. Who is the artist who shares his time between Middle Tennessee and New England, and has painted the portraits of several of Tennessee's more recent governors, which hang in the capitol building?

A. Martin Kellogg.

———◆———

Q. What former Tennessean is known as the official "Mule" artist?

A. Bonnie Shields.

SPORTS & LEISURE

C H A P T E R   F I V E

Q. What Tennessean was the winner of three gold medals in Olympic track competition in 1960?

A. Wilma Rudolph.

Q. The world's largest artificial ski surface is located where?

A. Gatlinburg.

Q. Who is said to be Vanderbilt's top basketball player of all time?

A. Clyde Lee, (1964-66), the 6′9″ center who later became a player for the Philadelphia 76ers.

Q. What Tennessee zoo was the famous home of MGM's roaring lion until his death in 1944?

A. Memphis Zoo.

Q. What coveted trophies did Darrell Waltrip, stock car racer of Franklin, earn in 1981 and 1982?

A. Winston Cup.

Q. As 1973 began, what ball player from Memphis could boast a record for 2,127 major league games, owned a .290 lifetime batting average, had made 2,453 hits, and had played for Cincinnati, Cleveland, St. Louis, and California?

A. Vada Edward Pinson, Jr.

Q. What was the name of the University of Tennessee's first full-time salaried coach?

A. J. A. Pierce.

Q. The movie *Coal Miner's Daughter,* starring Sissy Spacek, is about the life of which female country music star?

A. Loretta Lynn.

Q. Jonesboro is noted for what annual festival?

A. National Storytelling Festival.

Q. What was one of Rachel Jackson's leisurely pastimes?

A. Pipe smoking.

Q. At what museum can passengers take a five-mile ride on a steam-driven train between a 1920s frame depot and a 1940s brick depot?

A. The Tennessee Valley Railroad Museum.

Q. What year did the University of Tennessee Vols first wear their now-famous orange jerseys?

A. 1922.

Q. What famous racehorse of Andrew Jackson's defeated Ploughboy in a two mile race at Clover Bottom on April 3, 1806?

A. Truxton.

———◆———

Q. What athlete who owns a sixty-acre farm outside Henning hit .315 in 149 major league games for the Chicago Cubs in 1970?

A. James Lucius Hickman.

———◆———

Q. What was the recorded attendance of the 1982 Knoxville World's Fair?

A. 11,127,786.

———◆———

Q. What professional ball player from Rogersville played in the 1932 World Series?

A. Robert E. "Bob" Smith.

———◆———

Q. Who holds the world's paper airplane endurance record, set in the Municipal Auditorium in Nashville on March 26, 1975?

A. William Harlan "Bill" Pryor, 15.0 seconds.

———◆———

Q. What Tennessee woman played on the United States basketball team at the World University Games in Moscow, in 1976 served as co-captain of the United States women's basketball team at the XXI Olympiad in Montreal, and went on to become the women's coach at the University of Tennessee?

A. Pat Head Summitt.

———◆———

Q. What was David Crockett's fine for getting into a fight at the Old Racetrack south of Huntingdon?

A. Six coonskins.

Q. In what city is the Forked Deer Festival held the weekend after Labor Day?

A. Jackson.

———◆———

Q. What was the directive from then Professor Nathan Dougherty given to Bob Neyland as he was handed the University of Tennessee coaching reins?

A. Even the score with Vanderbilt.

———◆———

Q. What is the sport based on the old time mountain shooting contests?

A. Turkey Shoot.

———◆———

Q. What professional ball player died in Jamestown in 1965 and holds the major league record for most doubles in one season (67) in 1931?

A. Earl W. Webb.

———◆———

Q. Which reservoir holds the world's record for smallmouth bass?

A. Dale Hollow Reservoir.

———◆———

Q. What famous coach has led the Tennessee State Tigerbelles to monumental victories?

A. Ed Temple.

———◆———

Q. What was the name of the Chinese junk on which world adventurer Richard Halliburton of Brownsville lost his life in 1939 while attempting a trans-Pacific crossing?

A. Sea Dragon.

Q. The magnificent cliffs of the Sequatchie Valley make the area around Dunlap one of the top three areas in the United States for what sport?

A. Hang gliding.

———◆———

Q. What family could rightfully claim the title of "Tennessee's First Football Family"?

A. The Majors: All-American John, the late Bill, and talented Bobby.

———◆———

Q. What Tennessee athlete was one of baseball's more knowledgeable pitching instructors and helped to develop such fine Yankee pitchers as Whitey Ford, Allie Reynolds, Vic Raschi, Ed Lopat, Mel Stottlemyre and Fritz Peterson?

A. Jim Turner.

———◆———

Q. Where is the Southeastern 500 held?

A. Bristol.

———◆———

Q. In the early 1920s, what Negro National League baseball team was formed in Nashville by Tom T. Wilson?

A. The Nashville Elite Giants.

———◆———

Q. What University of Tennessee basketball star was born behind the Iron Curtain, in the Rumanian city of Satu Mare?

A. Ernie Grunfeld.

———◆———

Q. How much money did J. B. Whitehead and B. F. Thomas of Chattanooga pay for their Coca-Cola franchise?

A. $1.00, which Asa Candler, owner of the rights to Coca-Cola, never bothered to collect.

Q. What was the nickname of Frank George Hahn, born in Nashville, who held many Cincinnati Reds club records and retained a locker at the Cincinnati ball park for thirty years after his retirement?

A. "Noodles."

Q. What writer-poet, born in Murfreesboro in 1880, became known as the Dean of American Sportswriters?

A. Grantland Rice.

Q. What theme amusement park is situated in Memphis?

A. Libertyland.

Q. What innovative University of Tennessee football coach came up with the low-cut shoe, the tearaway jersey and the six-man defensive line?

A. General Neyland.

Q. What is the name of the Vanderbilt playing field?

A. Dudley Field.

Q. What country music star owns several music publishing companies and is also a major stockholder in the Nashville Sounds baseball team?

A. Conway Twitty.

Q. In what year was the women's track coach of Tennessee State University, Ed Temple, inducted into the Black Athlete's Hall of Fame?

A. 1977.

Q. What was the amount of prize money the *Commercial Appeal* of Memphis offered to the first person to fly an airplane over the city?

A. $5,000.

＋

Q. What athlete from Memphis was center fielder for the St. Louis Cardinals for eleven years, missing three years for military service, and went on to be a coach for the Cardinals and the manager for the Philadelphia Phillies?

A. Terry Bluford Moore.

＋

Q. What years encompassed the Neyland era at the University of Tennessee?

A. 1926-52.

＋

Q. What was the name of the horse from Nashville that won the Long Island "race of the century"?

A. Peytona.

＋

Q. What Grand Ole Opry star, who was killed in a plane crash in Davidson County, at one time signed a contract to play baseball for the St. Louis Cardinals?

A. James Travis "Jim" Reeves.

＋

Q. What was a favorite Choctaw sporting event?

A. Stickball, an early form of lacrosse.

＋

Q. What was the cost of the Sunsphere, the Knoxvillle World's Fair theme structure?

A. $8.5 million.

Q. What Henderson County town was a noted gambling resort before the War Between the States?

A. Pleasant Exchange.

Q. Who was the first real Tigerbelle star, known as the "Mother of the Tigerbelles"?

A. Aeriwentha Mae Faggs.

Q. What Vanderbilt star center was named the SEC Most Valuable player in basketball in 1988?

A. Will Purdue.

Q. What Knoxville-born basketball player was voted All-American and All-Missouri Valley Conference twice?

A. Paul Hogue.

Q. Where are the National Field Trials for Bird Dogs held each year?

A. Grand Junction.

Q. Who did coach Bob Neyland of the Vols say was the greatest player he had ever coached?

A. Gene McEver, who played in 1928, '29 and '31.

Q. What is the second longest-running live program in the history of radio?

A. *The Waking Crew*, WSM Nashville.

Q. The corkscrew roller coaster at Opryland, known as the Wabash Cannonball, races on a 1,200-foot-long track at what speed?

A. 50 mph.

Q. Memorial Gymnasium on the Vanderbilt campus was built as a memorial to whom?

A. The alumni who died in World War II.

Q. What was Dean N. W. Dougherty of the University of Tennessee referring to when he said, "the best move I ever made"?

A. The hiring of Robert Reese Neyland to the coaching staff.

Q. In 1929 the state legislature removed what laws governing highways in Tennessee?

A. Speed limit laws.

Q. What Tennessee State sprinters qualified for the 1956 United States Olympic team?

A. Mae Faggs, Isabelle Daniels, Margaret Matthews, Lucinda Williams, Willye B. White and Wilma Rudolph.

Q. Who was the Tennessean who won the American Gold Cup, the richest horse jumping contest in the world?

A. Melanie Smith.

Q. All-American basketball player Richard Fuqua, born in Chattanooga, carried what nickname?

A. The Mad Bomber.

Q. What major league ball player from Memphis played for the St. Louis Cardinals, maintaining a batting average of .295, with 14 homers, and 69 RBI's in 1967?

A. Tim McCarver.

Q. When did the first real prominence come to the University of Tennessee football team?

A. 1914, with the Volunteers defeat of Vanderbilt.

Q. One of the lions housed at the Memphis zoo played opposite what famous movie actor?

A. Johnny Weissmuller in *Tarzan's Secret Treasure*.

Q. What is the highest underground waterfall and deepest commercial cavern in the United States open to the public?

A. Ruby Falls.

Q. Old Hickory Reservoir sports the world's record for what type of fish?

A. Walleye.

Q. What illness prohibited Roy Acuff from accepting an invitation by the New York Yankees to attend their spring training camp in 1930?

A. A serious sunstroke.

Q. Who is the film and movie director who attended Vanderbilt University and currently serves on its Board?

A. Delbert Mann.

Q. What is the name of the football stadium at the University of Tennessee in Knoxville?

A. Neyland Stadium.

Q. Where is the annual Iroquois Steeplechase held?

A. Percy Warner Park in Nashville.

Q. What professional ball player of Chattanooga was known as "Daddy Wags" and "Cheeks"?

A. Leon L. Wagner.

Q. The Okra Festival is celebrated in what town?

A. Bells.

Q. The antique carousel which is approximately 100 years old was stored for nearly fifty years in 5,000 unmarked pieces in what country before coming to Opryland?

A. Denmark.

Q. What great athlete was the twentieth of twenty-two children and as a child had scarlet fever, whooping cough and polio?

A. Wilma Rudolph.

Q. In 1987, what Tennessee State University outside linebacker was the third round draft pick of the New York Jets?

A. Onzy Elam.

Q. What was the career coaching record of Jesse Neely, who was captain of the Commodore football team, coached several university teams, and became athletic director at Vanderbilt?

A. 207-99-14.

———◆———

Q. In what city is the $31 million Tennessee Aquarium situated?

A. Chattanooga.

———◆———

Q. What is the name of the nine-day festival held in Memphis each year to dramatize the world's largest cotton market?

A. Cotton Carnival.

———◆———

Q. What Columbia pitcher won 157 National League games and made 114 pinch hits in 16 major league seasons, and played second base for the Boston Braves during the 1924 and 1925 seasons?

A. Charles Fred "Red" Lucas.

———◆———

Q. What race was won in 1910 by a horse named Donau, owned by Nashville beer-maker William Gerst?

A. The Kentucky Derby.

———◆———

Q. What Tennessee university won a 1990 CFA award for graduating 70 percent of its football players within five years?

A. Vanderbilt.

———◆———

Q. What was the name of the field first used by football players at the University of Tennessee?

A. Wait Field.

Q. Why was Opryland's showboat named the *General Jackson*?

A. It was named after the first steamboat to operate on the Cumberland River.

———◆———

Q. What land developer was responsible for the "See Rock City" barns?

A. Garnet Carter.

———◆———

Q. What University of Tennessee football player known as "Big Un" was captain of three varsity athletic teams, one of the first Tennessee players to make the All-Southern team, chairman of the University of Tennessee Athletic Council from 1917 to 1956, and vice president of the National Football Foundation's Hall of Fame?

A. Nathan Washington Dougherty.

———◆———

Q. Who was the All-American basketball player, born in Jefferson City, who earned the title "The Man with the Golden Arm"?

A. A. W. Davis.

———◆———

Q. What Memphis Red Sox player was the first black pitcher to sign with the major leagues (Brooklyn Dodgers)?

A. Dan Bankhead.

———◆———

Q. Meadow Park Lake, located southwest of Crossville, is the scene of what annual races?

A. Dixie Outboard Motor Boat Association Competition.

———◆———

Q. At what state park is the Mountaineer Folk Festival held?

A. Fall Creek Falls State Park.

Q. By decree of House Bill 620 of 1980, what became the official state dance?

A. Square Dance.

Q. In the 1956 Austrian Olympics, only six medals were won by women athletes; how many were won by Tennessee State Tigerbelles?

A. Five.

Q. In 1987, what University of Tennessee football player was the second to rush more than 1000 yards in a season?

A. Reggie Cobb.

Q. What exposition did Knoxville host in 1910?

A. Appalachian Conservation Exposition.

Q. What year did cigar-smoking "Big" John Merritt become head football coach of Tennessee State University?

A. 1963.

Q. During what weekend is the "Cherokee Day of Recognition" held each year at the Red Clay State Historic Area?

A. First weekend in August.

Q. What year was University of Tennessee football coach Johnny Majors elected to the National Football Foundation Hall of Fame?

A. 1987.

Q. What is the state record for a blue catfish?

A. 130 pounds, at Ft. Loudon Reservoir.

Q. What men made up the "Three Musketeers" coaching staff of the University of Tennessee in 1926?

A. Paul Parker, Bob Neyland and Bill Britton.

Q. What noted NASCAR Grand National circuit driver is a resident of Franklin?

A. Darrell Waltrip.

Q. What was the name of the first minor league baseball team in Nashville, formed in 1901 in the Southern Association?

A. The Vols.

Q. Mr. Preston Dorris is noted for what transportation first in Nashville in 1896?

A. Driving the first automobile in the city.

Q. What Memphis ball player played in 180 major league games, managed and was part owner of the Memphis team and then pulled out of baseball in 1947?

A. James Thompson "Doc" Prothro.

Q. Where is the Tom Thumb Course, the world's first miniature golf course?

A. Lookout Mountain.

Q. What great aviation pioneer brought the first "flying circus" to Tennessee at the Memphis Fairgrounds in 1910?

A. Glenn Curtiss.

Q. Roan Mountain is the site of what colorful event?

A. The Rhododendron Festival.

Q. Who was the 6' 7" forward, born in Middleton in 1937, who became the top basketball player in Mississippi State University history?

A. Bailey Howell.

Q. What well-known racehorse won the 1949 Iroquois Steeplechase?

A. Fatal Interview.

Q. What was the first fee for a driver's license in the state?

A. Fifty cents a year.

Q. The "Vols" of the University of Tennessee won their first Southern championship in what year?

A. 1914.

Q. What man managed the Cleveland Indians in 1957?

A. Major Kerby Farrell of Leapwood, Tennessee.

Q. What festival is held each August in South Fulton to promote friendship with Latin American countries?

A. International Banana Festival.

Q. What University of Tennessee player under Coach Bob Neyland later gained coaching fame at Yale and West Point?

A. Beattie Feathers.

Q. What was the name of the "gay nineties" resort in Anderson County that consisted of 150 rooms and four stories and attracted the well-to-do of this country and Europe?

A. Oliver Springs Hotel.

Q. Where is the annual Choctaw Indian Pow Wow held?

A. Chucalissa, a reconstructed Indian village near Memphis.

Q. Ted "Houndog" McClain, born in Nashville in 1948, played his first pro season with what team?

A. Carolina Cougars.

Q. Tennessee State University set what first for a school in the 1956 Olympics?

A. Became the first school or club to have six members qualify for Olympic competition.

Q. What now retired Nashville businessman was owner of the Birmingham Black Barons in 1954 and 1955?

A. William "Soo" Bridgeforth.

Q. Who was the two-time Grammy Award-winning country music star who was also a stock car racer?

A. Martin David "Marty Robbins" Robinson.

◆

Q. Who was the coach at the University of Tennessee in 1907 when Tennessee won its game in Atlanta against Georgia Tech but was declared the loser after the game was completed?

A. Coach George Levene.

◆

Q. What Tennessee State Tiger won a gold medal in the long jump in the 1960 Rome Olympics?

A. Ralph Boston.

◆

Q. What national television program in January of 1957 aired a special entitled "Clinton and the Law," dealing with school integration problems in Clinton?

A. *See It Now*, Edward R. Murrow's CBS-TV program.

◆

Q. What professional ball player, nicknamed "Gomer," from Caney Springs played for the old Washington Senators in the 1960s, then played for the Los Angeles Dodgers?

A. Claude Wilson Osteen, pitcher.

◆

Q. In what year did Jesse Neely captain the Vanderbilt Commodore football team?

A. 1922.

◆

Q. What was the nickname given to pitcher Jim Turner of Antioch, who played professional baseball and also was a pitching instructor for the New York Yankees?

A. "Milkman."

Q. What is the name of the motel chain headquartered in Memphis that is the largest in the world?

A. Holiday Inn.

———◆———

Q. What was the mile pacing record set in 1938 by the horse Billy Direct from Maury County?

A. 1:55.

———◆———

Q. On November 27, 1890, the first game of college football in Nashville was played at Sulphur Dell between which two Nashville colleges?

A. Peabody and Vanderbilt.

———◆———

Q. What nationally-known sportswriter from Nashville penned these words: "For when the One Great Scorer comes to write against your name, He writes not that you won or lost, but how you played the game"?

A. Grantland Rice.

———◆———

Q. In what city is the National Sport Fishing Center located?

A. Chattanooga.

———◆———

Q. What Coalfield athlete played in the major leagues, then became coach for the Washington Senators in 1961-71, and, when the Senators changed to the Texas Rangers during the winter of 1971-72, remained as coach through the 1972 season?

A. Sidney Charles Hudson.

———◆———

Q. The early resort located at Montvale Springs in Blount County often was given what title?

A. The Saratoga of the South.

Q. What was the name of the horse from Belle Meade stock farm in Nashville that in 1881 became the first American-bred horse to win the English Derby?

A. Iroquois.

———◆———

Q. Where is the Tennessee Renaissance Festival held each June?

A. Castle Gwyn, Triune.

———◆———

Q. What baseball player born in Gordonsville was a scout for the New York Mets during the years 1963-68?

A. Tommy Bridges.

———◆———

Q. What university employs the state's fifth largest police force?

A. Vanderbilt.

———◆———

Q. What was the name of the town in which the Old Deery Inn, which hosted many distinguished travelers in the early days, was situated?

A. Blountville.

———◆———

Q. Who was responsible for the University of Tennessee changing its football jerseys from the original black jersey with orange and white bands on the sleeves to orange jerseys with white numerals?

A. Pap Striegel, player and later member of the University of Tennessee Athletic Council.

———◆———

Q. What nationally-known candy made in Tennessee consists of chocolate, caramel, peanuts, and marshmallow and is named for the pleasing sound made by a small child?

A. Goo Goo.

Q. What pitcher was professional baseball's first woman to be signed to a contract and in an exhibition game struck out Babe Ruth and Lou Gehrig in succession?

A. Jackie Mitchell, signed by Chattanooga in April, 1931.

Q. How many miles of well-stocked trout streams are found in the Great Smoky Mountains National Park?

A. 600 miles.

Q. Who was Tennessee's first full-fledged all-American in football and also was the first Vol elected to the National Football Foundation Hall of Fame?

A. Gene McEver.

Q. When did The Nashville Network begin operation?

A. March, 1983.

Q. What was the name of the mile harness track in Memphis that hosted many famous horses?

A. North Memphis Driving Park.

Q. Who received the first drivers license in the state?

A. Sergeant Jimmy Phelps of the Tennessee Highway Patrol.

Q. What man who had served in two previous Olympics was chosen to be the United States women's track and field coach in the 1980 Olympics?

A. Coach Ed Temple, Tennessee State University.

Q. Annie Taylor, honor student from the Tennessee School for the Deaf, won a silver medal in the 1977 Deaf Olympics held at Bucharest, Romania, for what event?

A. High jump, 5′3¾″.

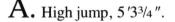

Q. In 1988, what Tennessee high school football team was ranked by *USA Today* as being one of the top ten high school teams in the nation?

A. Brentwood Academy.

Q. What Sparta-born ball player played in the 1933 World Series?

A. Walter C. "Lefty" Stewart, Washington Senators.

Q. Bolivar is noted for what annual celebration?

A. Tennessee Forest Festival.

Q. Where is the International Banana Festival, which features a one-ton banana pudding, held each September?

A. South Fulton.

Q. What is the seating capacity of the Opry House?

A. 4,400.

Q. What Tigerbelle won the gold medal in the 200-meter dash at the 1964 Tokyo Olympics?

A. Edith McGuire.

Q. What professional baseball team of the 1920s became one of the nation's top ten black teams and won the championship in 1938?

A. The Red Sox of Memphis.

Q. What Tigerbelle won a gold medal in the 1964 Tokyo Olympics for the 100-meter dash, and in the 1968 Mexico City Olympics won two gold medals, one in the women's 400 meter relay and the other in the 100-meter dash?

A. Wyomia Tyus.

Q. Roan Mountain State Park holds what special honor?

A. The South's only cross-country ski resort state park.

Q. What is Tennessee's oldest continual professional baseball team?

A. The Chattanooga Lookouts.

Q. What was the name of the horse foaled in 1889 in Williamson County that became the first harness horse to go a mile in less than two minutes?

A. Star Pointer.

Q. Grand Ole Opry performers at the Ryman Auditorium took their breaks at what lounge?

A. Tootsie's Orchid Lounge.

Q. What athlete played football for the Los Angeles Rams and Chicago Bears after graduating from Vanderbilt?

A. Bill Wade.

Q. What champion automobile race driver worked with the famous aviators, the Moisant brothers, in the Memphis area?

A. Barney Oldfield.

———◆———

Q. As of 1991, how many times have the University of Tennessee Volunteers been to the Sugar Bowl?

A. Seven (1941, 1943, 1952, 1957, 1971, 1986, 1991).

———◆———

Q. During what years was Bowden Wyatt football coach at the University of Tennessee?

A. 1955-62.

———◆———

Q. What university, known for losing a football game 222-0, revived its football program in 1990 after an absence of 41 years?

A. Cumberland.

———◆———

Q. By what nickname is Middle Tennessee State University's football team known?

A. The Blue Raiders.

———◆———

Q. In what Tennessee race did England's Princess Anne make her U.S. horse racing debut in 1987?

A. The Royal Chase at Percy Warner Park.

———◆———

Q. What Nashville-born forward was with Minnesota, Miami, New York, Kentucky, and Memphis and was nicknamed "Big Game"?

A. Les Hunter.

Q. Where is the Tennessee Walking Horse National Celebration held annually?

A. Shelbyville.

Q. At what age did Alabama graduate Bill Battle become head football coach at the University of Tennessee?

A. 28.

Q. Columbia hosts what annual spring event in honor of a southern tradition?

A. Mule Day.

Q. What three Tigerbelles qualified to be in the 1980 summer Olympic Games in Moscow?

A. Chandra Cheeseborough, Brenda Moorehead and Kathy McMillan.

Q. What Linden-born ball player signed with the Washington Senators in 1907 and stayed with the club most of his life?

A. Jess Clyde "Deerfoot" Milan.

Q. For what event did Wilma Rudolph win her first Gold Medal in the 1960 Olympics at Rome?

A. 100-meter dash which she ran in 11 seconds flat.

Q. What ball player born in Mulberry played for the Detroit Tigers and Washington Senators, but had to cut his career short because of tuberculosis?

A. Jonathan T. "Rocky" Stone.

Q. Noted pianist and studio musician, Floyd Cramer, is host to what sporting event each year?

A. Republic Airlines' Floyd Cramer Golf Classic.

———◆———

Q. You are not required to have a fishing license in the state if you are under what age or over what age?

A. Under 16 or over 65.

———◆———

Q. What is the name of the Memphis zoo?

A. Overton Park Zoo.

———◆———

Q. Who was the first black head coach of a major sport in the SEC?

A. Wade Houston (Tennessee).

———◆———

Q. In the sport of bow hunting, one's bow must be capable of propelling a hunting arrow what distance to be considered legal in Tennessee?

A. 150 yards.

———◆———

Q. What type of water craft has a higher number of registrations in Tennessee than in any other state?

A. Houseboats.

———◆———

Q. Where is the Danny Thomas Classic held each year?

A. Memphis, at the Colonial Country Club.

Q. What celebration is held each year in Gatlinburg, featuring parades, ice skating shows, skiing, and a formal ball?

A. The Twelve Days of Christmas.

Q. What is the only Tennessee river to feature Class V white water?

A. The Ocoee.

Q. How many campers use the state's camping facilities each year?

A. More than four million.

Q. The Pat Boone Bethel Celebrity Golf Tournament is held in which city?

A. Chattanooga.

Q. In 1981, what two teams played the first AA game to be broadcast nationwide?

A. The Nashville Sounds and the Columbus Astros.

Q. Which four Tennessee rivers are noted for great float trips?

A. Hiwassee, Harpeth, Duck and Buffalo rivers.

Q. What is the name of the area in downtown Nashville known for its concentration of nightclubs?

A. Printer's Alley.

Q. Who is the Middle Tennessee swimmer who "brought home the gold" from the 1984 Olympics?

A. Tracy Caulkins.

Q. Where may you ride an elephant in Tennessee?

A. The Knoxville Zoological Park.

Q. How many state parks are there in Tennessee?

A. 38.

Q. What is the length of the Ober Gatlinburg Tramway?

A. 2.2 miles.

Q. Nashville hosts what golf tournament each year?

A. Music City Pro-Celebrity Tournament.

Q. The world's steepest incline railway is found in which city?

A. Chattanooga.

Q. What are the four major league farm teams in Tennessee?

A. Knoxville Blue Jays, Chattanooga Lookouts, Nashville Sounds, and Memphis Chicks.

SCIENCE & NATURE

CHAPTER SIX

Q. On what type of tree in Washington County did Daniel Boone carve "D. Boone cilled a bar in year 1760?"

A. Beech tree.

Q. What is the Tennessee state flower?

A. Iris.

Q. Where in Tennessee would you find exhibits on the peaceful uses of nuclear energy?

A. The American Museum of Science and Energy, Oak Ridge.

Q. What was the first crop raised by settlers in Middle Tennessee?

A. Corn.

Q. What breed of horse was originally bred for planters and overseers to ride while directing work in their fields?

A. The plantation walking horse.

Q. What three types of poisonous snakes are indigenous to Tennessee?

A. Copperhead, cottonmouth and rattlesnake.

Q. During which month do the dogwood trees usually bloom in Tennessee?

A. April.

Q. What Tennessean made history aboard the seven-day flight of the space shuttle *Discovery*?

A. Dr. Rhea Seddon, Murfreesboro.

Q. What substance accounts for the greatest mining income in Tennessee?

A. Coal.

Q. What marks the western limits of the Highland Rim area of the state?

A. The western valley of the Tennessee River.

Q. What is the Tennessee state bird?

A. Mockingbird.

Q. During which geological period were the coal fields of Tennessee created?

A. Pennsylvanian Period.

Q. Who developed a device to electrocute cockroaches while living in Memphis in 1866 and 1867?

A. Thomas Edison.

◆

Q. Where in Tennessee are the world-famous Cretaceous marine fossil deposits to be found?

A. Coon Creek in McNairy County.

◆

Q. What state agency formed in 1903 is responsible for administering wildlife in the state?

A. Game and Fish Department.

◆

Q. What lady came to Pleasant Hill in 1917 with a dream for better rural health and gained the title "Doctor woman of the Cumberlands"?

A. May Cravath Wharton.

◆

Q. Large quantities of plateau bituminous coal were processed into coke, which serves what use in the production of pig iron?

A. The deoxidizing agent in a blast furnace.

◆

Q. What flower was the Tennessee State Flower until 1933 and, according to legend, resembles the instruments of Christ's crucifixion?

A. Passionflower (now the State Wildflower).

◆

Q. In 1867 David M. Brandenbury was the first to establish what type of large-scale operation in Tennessee?

A. Strawberry farming.

Q. In 1851 wool from the sheep of agriculturalist Mark Robertson Cockrill won first place in what competition?

A. The World's Fair in London.

———◆———

Q. What federal project was the first to be constructed under the National Environmental Policy Act?

A. The Tennessee–Tombigbee Waterway.

———◆———

Q. In response to the need for gun powder and explosives for the war effort in Europe, what company located a large munitions plant at Old Hickory in 1917?

A. The DuPont Company.

———◆———

Q. Which four prominent groups of fossils are found in Cambrian rocks in Tennessee?

A. Brachiopods, gastropods, graptolites and trilobites.

———◆———

Q. What is the state's only native bamboo?

A. Switch cane (*Arundinaria michx*).

———◆———

Q. In what county is the natural lake Clear Lake to be found?

A. Carroll County.

———◆———

Q. To how many consumers is TVA power distributed?

A. Over 2.7 million consumers.

Q. What marsupial native to Tennessee is considered a delicacy to rural and mountain folk when cooked with sweet potatoes?

A. Oppossum.

Q. What three songbirds are commonly found in Tennessee?

A. Wood thrush, mockingbird and robin.

Q. What made the clock in the Union Station tower in Nashville unique at the time of its construction?

A. It was digital, with numerals mounted on movable cloth strips.

Q. What is the most abundant Mississippian fossil found in Tennessee?

A. Crinoid.

Q. What mineral that sold for ten dollars a bushel was in great demand for preserving and seasoning food in the pioneer days of Tennessee?

A. Salt.

Q. Who was a professor of surgery at the University of Nashville in 1851-1861 and 1870-1877 and served as president of the American Medical Association in 1857-58?

A. Paul Fitzsimons Eve.

Q. What noisy insect becomes a pest in the state about every thirteen years?

A. Cicada.

Q. What insect crossed into the United States from Mexico around 1890 and caused millions of dollars in damages to cotton crops, not only in Tennessee but throughout the Southeastern area?

A. Boll weevil.

Q. What is the most common vulture in Tennessee?

A. Turkey vulture.

Q. During the excavation of the site for the First American Center in Nashville, the fossilized bones of what animal were found?

A. A sabre-toothed tiger.

Q. Under which president's administration was the Tennessee Valley Authority formed in 1933?

A. Franklin D. Roosevelt.

Q. Augustin Gattinger, noted botanist, published what classic work in the field of botany?

A. *Tennessee Flora*, published in 1887.

Q. Tobacco is Tennessee's second largest cash crop; what is the third?

A. Cotton.

Q. What archeological treasures found in a Tennessee cave in 1982 are unique to North America?

A. Thirteenth-century mud drawings.

Q. Which three diseases took the greatest number of lives in early urban centers in the state?

A. Cholera, yellow fever and small pox.

———◆———

Q. How many kinds of flowering plants are found in the Great Smoky Mountains?

A. More than 1,300.

———◆———

Q. What is the state animal?

A. Raccoon.

———◆———

Q. The Tennessee Coal, Iron and Railroad Company was the largest coal producer in the state in 1882 and produced how many tons of coal that year?

A. 360,000 tons.

———◆———

Q. The first electric street car in Nashville made its inaugural trip on what date?

A. April 30, 1889.

———◆———

Q. The red spruce trees (*Picea rubens sarg.*) of the mountains of East Tennessee sometimes attain what age?

A. 350 years.

———◆———

Q. Who first imported Jersey cattle from the Channel Islands into Tennessee?

A. Campbell Brown, M. C. Campbell and W. J. Webster of Maury County.

Q. What research center has developed three new designs for wheelchairs?

A. University of Tennessee, Memphis.

———◆———

Q. A mill built by the Shields Brothers in 1820 on Spring Creek was one of the first of its kind to produce what product west of the Appalachian Divide?

A. Paper.

———◆———

Q. John W. Dodge, who moved from New York to Nashville and purchased 5,000 acres of land in Cumberland County, planted much of this acreage in what type of trees?

A. Apple (some 82,000 trees).

———◆———

Q. Why is the Memphis mansion the "Pink Palace" called by that name?

A. It is made of pink Georgia marble.

———◆———

Q. In whose honor is the highest mountain in Tennessee named?

A. Thomas Laiver Clingman.

———◆———

Q. In what city did Sharp Electronics build its first U.S. plant?

A. Memphis.

———◆———

Q. What was the original name of Tennessee Valley Authority's Norris Dam project?

A. Cove Creek Dam.

Q. What dangerous game animal was introduced to the states by wealthy English sportsmen in 1912?

A. The Russian wild boar.

———◆———

Q. Who was the native Nashvillian celestial photographer and astronomer who discovered the fifth moon of Jupiter in 1892?

A. Edward E. Barnard.

———◆———

Q. Small coal mines in East Tennessee operated by farmers during the winter months are referred to as what?

A. Snowbird mines.

———◆———

Q. Where was the state's first heart transplant performed?

A. St. Thomas Hospital, Nashville.

———◆———

Q. The bark of which three trees was used by the early settlers to produce dyes?

A. Hickory, walnut and maple.

———◆———

Q. Mud Island in Memphis is the site of what museum?

A. Mississippi River Museum.

———◆———

Q. What bird that is now extinct used to roost in large numbers near Memphis?

A. The passenger pigeon.

Q. In what community did the extensive cutting of forests, sulphurous fumes from smelters, and erosion of topsoil create a fifty-square-mile moonscape-like, barren terrain?

A. Copperhill.

———◆———

Q. Paul Linde of Crossville is noted for handcrafting what type of optical instruments?

A. Telescopes.

———◆———

Q. What is the state tree of Tennessee?

A. Tulip poplar.

———◆———

Q. What is the largest marble building in the world constructed of Knox County marble?

A. The National Gallery of Art, Washington, D.C.

———◆———

Q. What is the general elevation of the Cumberland Plateau?

A. 1,700 to 1,900 feet.

———◆———

Q. Who established the Mercy Hospital, now Hubbard Hospital, in Nashville specifically for the care of blacks?

A. Dr. Robert Felton Boyd.

———◆———

Q. How many species of salamanders have been recorded in the Great Smokies?

A. Twenty-six species, more than are found in any other place in the world.

Q. What fungus, scientifically known as *discula,* is threatening the dogwoods in Bradley County?

A. Dogwood anthracnose.

———◆———

Q. For what did Dr. Earl W. Sutherland, research biologist of Vanderbilt University, win a Nobel Prize in 1971?

A. For "opening new paths of research in diabetes and cancer."

———◆———

Q. Tennessean Marion Dorset implemented what program for the U.S.D.A.?

A. Meat inspection.

———◆———

Q. The Cherokee Indians who occupied much of East Tennessee called which bird their "great sacred bird"?

A. The eagle.

———◆———

Q. Which woman legislator introduced the bill to purchase the first Smokies property by the state of Tennessee and after that was known as "mother of the Great Smoky Mountains National Park"?

A. Annie May Davis.

———◆———

Q. What Murfreesboro landmark features a medical museum?

A. Oaklands.

———◆———

Q. Who founded the first thoroughbred nursery in the United States?

A. William Giles Harding.

Q. What are the state insects of Tennessee?

A. The firefly and the lady bug.

Q. What three types of Magnolia trees are found in the Great Smoky Mountains National Park?

A. Umbrella Magnolia (*Magnolia tripetala*), Cucumber Tree (*Magnolia acuminata*) and Fraser Magnolia (*Magnolia fraseri*).

Q. Which Mississippian rocks contain fossil remains of fish?

A. Maury shale and Newman limestone.

Q. What were the six main crops grown by the Cherokees?

A. Corn, beans, squash, sunflowers, pumpkins and gourds.

Q. What event in 1821 in Lawrence County destroyed David Crockett's grist mill, powder mill and distillery, forcing him into bankruptcy?

A. The flooding of Shoal Creek.

Q. What is the meaning of the Creek Indian name *Chatunuga* given to Lookout Mountain?

A. "Rock which comes to an end."

Q. What park is the site of the second largest Indian mound in the United States?

A. Pinson Mounds Archeological Park.

Q. For what purpose does the Japanese cultured pearl industry import Tennessee pigtoe mussel shells?

A. For use as nuclei for growing cultured pearls.

Q. Middle and East Tennessee Ordovician Period rocks contain some of the world's most important deposits of what mineral?

A. Zinc.

Q. What material was gathered along the southern end of the Natchez Trace to be utilized by Tennesseans for stuffing mattresses?

A. Spanish moss.

Q. Ducks and geese migrate to which two lakes in huge numbers?

A. Reelfoot Lake and Kentucky Lake.

Q. What is Tennessee's chief manufacturing industry?
A. Chemicals.

Q. What is the name of the highly publicized natural bridge in Wayne County?

A. The Courthouse.

Q. What was finally discovered to be the cause of milk sickness, a disease that caused much hardship for early livestock farmers in East Tennessee?

A. Ingestion of tremetol, a poison found in the white snakeroot plant.

Q. What was one of the major reasons for selecting the Oak Ridge area for atomic research?

A. The abundant energy supply available through Tennessee Valley Authority.

———◆———

Q. What three types of squirrels are found in Tennessee?

A. Red, gray and flying.

———◆———

Q. For what item in 1796 did George James become the first Tennessean to receive a patent?

A. A salt manufacturing device, by an evaporation process.

———◆———

Q. What county is renowned for its orchards and nurseries?

A. Warren County.

———◆———

Q. What famous television personality helped found St. Jude's Children Hospital of Memphis in 1958?

A. Danny Thomas.

———◆———

Q. How far below the earth's surface is Ruby Falls situated?

A. 1,120 feet.

———◆———

Q. What is now housed in the Clarence Saunder's Pink Palace?

A. It is now the Pink Palace Museum in Memphis, an educational facility for natural history.

Q. What was a common native ore used in the 1800s to produce iron?

A. Brown hematite.

Q. In 1980, what university won the Koerper Award for outstanding professionalism, awarded by the National Society of Professional Engineers?

A. Tennessee State University.

Q. What island in the Mississippi River at Memphis was formed by an eddy depositing mud and gravel against the stern of the gunboat *Aphrodite* anchored there for several months in 1910 due to low water?

A. Mud Island.

Q. What were small locomotives used around coal mines and coal washers called?

A. Dinkies.

Q. In 1990 what computer firm did North American Philips move from Great Neck, New York, to Knoxville?

A. Headstart Technologies.

Q. What is the name of the present-day relative of the crinoid, which appeared first in shallow seas covering parts of Tennessee during the Silurian geological period?

A. Sea lily.

Q. The topographical area of West Tennessee is called the Coastal Plain because it was covered by a shallow sea during what geological age?

A. Late Cretaceous and Tertiary Periods.

Q. Who owned the first seeing-eye dog in the United States?

A. Morris Frank of Nashville.

———◆———

Q. During August, what type of bird roosts by the thousands in the area of the intersection of Tennessee highways 95 and 62?

A. Purple martin.

———◆———

Q. Paul Fitzsimmons Eve, professor of surgery at the University of Nashville, was the first American doctor to perform what type of surgery?

A. A hysterectomy.

———◆———

Q. What are the thick deposits of glacially derived wind-blown material found in West Tennessee called?

A. Loess.

———◆———

Q. What causes the formation of sinkholes in Tennessee?

A. The collapse of underground caverns.

———◆———

Q. Four rare plants—the linear-leaved gentian, mountain krigia, three-forked rush and Cain's reedgrass—are only known to be found where in Tennessee?

A. Mount Le Conte.

———◆———

Q. The McClung Museum featuring exhibits on anthropology, archaeology, science and natural history is located on which university campus?

A. University of Tennessee, Knoxville.

Q. What is the name of the endangered fishing eagle that is making a comeback in Tennessee?

A. Osprey.

———◆———

Q. What is the lowest temperature ever recorded in Tennessee?

A. -32 degrees Fahrenheit (Dec. 30, 1917, Mountain City).

———◆———

Q. What 7,000-acre high-tech industrial park is trying to start a Tennessee equivalent to California's Silicon Valley?

A. The Tennessee Technology Corridor (East Tennessee).

———◆———

Q. What type of tree is most prevalent on the summit of Clingman's Dome?

A. Fraser fir (*Abies fraseri*).

———◆———

Q. The aluminum reduction North Plant at Alcoa, the largest plant under one roof in the world when completed in 1941, covered how many acres?

A. 55 acres.

———◆———

Q. What is the state gem of Tennessee?

A. Natural pearls from the rivers of the state.

———◆———

Q. What is the name of the geophysical features of East Tennessee created by one of the largest anticline formations in the world?

A. Sequatchie Valley.

Q. How many major Tennessee Valley Authority dams harness the Tennessee River watershed?

A. 23.

———◆———

Q. What is Tennessee's largest cash crop?

A. Soybeans.

———◆———

Q. A smelting works was opened in 1881 in Clinton to processs what type of ore?

A. Zinc ore.

———◆———

Q. Giles Christopher Savage served in what capacity at Vanderbilt University from 1886 to 1911?

A. Professor of Opthalmology.

———◆———

Q. Who was the high priestess of the Cherokees who is credited with introducing milk cows to her people?

A. Nancy Ward.

———◆———

Q. The underlying limestones of the Sequatchie Valley are of which geological age?

A. Ordovician Age.

———◆———

Q. What tree is shown upon the flag of the governor of the state of Tennessee?

A. A hickory tree.

Q. In 1943 the Clinton Engineer Works in Oak Ridge played an essential role in what government endeavor?

A. The Manhattan Project, which produced the atomic bomb.

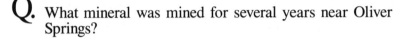

Q. What is the approximate population of white-tailed deer in Tennessee?

A. 350,000.

Q. What mineral was mined for several years near Oliver Springs?

A. Salt.

Q. What professor of geology and minerology at the University of Tennessee from 1869 to 1875 is noted for having discovered a new species of trilobite in New York state?

A. Frank Howe Bradley.

Q. What are the only two known sites for the White Water-Crowfoot plant in Tennessee?

A. Radnor Lake Natural Area in Nashville and the Highland Rim.

Q. In what county are the last two wild cranberry bogs to be found?

A. Johnson County.

Q. Gene Hyde of Jackson plants groves of pecans using seeds from what historic tree?

A. The Natchez Trace Pecan.

Q. Approximately how long ago did the wooly mammoth and sabre-toothed cats disappear from Tennessee?

A. Ten thousand years ago.

Q. Where is the world's largest stand of rhododendron bushes?

A. Roan Mountain State Park.

Q. What lady from Meharry Medical College in Nashville became the first black woman to practice general surgery in the South?

A. Dr. Dorothy Brown.

Q. During which geological period did corals appear in Tennessee?

A. Ordovician period.

Q. What river in the state is the largest tributary of the Ohio River?

A. The Tennessee River.

Q. Henry Horton State Park is in what county?

A. Marshall County.

Q. The Middle Tennessee Experiment Station, a model farming and land reclamation center, is in what Maury County community?

A. Neapolis.

Q. What was the death toll in Memphis from the yellow fever epedemic of 1878?

A. 5,152 fatalities.

Q. The most regular wintering site for golden eagles in Tennessee is in what county?

A. Cannon County.

Q. What new unit was introduced to the Tennessee Highway Patrol in 1978?

A. K-9 Unit.

Q. What are lakes along the Mississippi River that are created by meandering of the river channel called?

A. Oxbow lakes.

Q. Of what were early log cabin floors made?

A. Hard-packed dirt.

Q. What colorful building material is quarried around Crab Orchard?

A. Crab Orchard sandstone.

Q. In what year was the atomic energy plant built in Oak Ridge?

A. 1942.

Q. George R. Dempster, an experienced contractor and mechanic, who also served as Knoxville City Manager and one term as mayor, developed what product that became an important Knoxville industry?

A. The Dempster "Dumpster," a large portable container used to collect and remove quantities of trash.

Q. What commodity in the Memphis area was known as "white gold"?

A. Cotton.

Q. Norris Reservoir covers how many acres of land?

A. 34,000.

Q. What is the major coal mining technique used in East Tennessee?

A. Strip mining.

Q. What extensive cave system is found near McMinnville?

A. Cumberland Caverns.

Q. What was the name of the salt and sulphur spring that attracted game animals of all kinds to the area of present-day Nashville?

A. Great French Lick.

Q. What provided the power for the early grist mills across the state?

A. Water.

Q. What lake in the northwestern part of the state was formed by earthquakes in the winter of 1811-12?

A. Reelfoot Lake.

———◆———

Q. The often dangerous work of removing of supportive pillars of coal from mines in which all the rest of the coal had been removed was called what?

A. Robbing.

———◆———

Q. Who was the famous naturalist who arrived near Memphis in December of 1820 and noted sighting gulls, cormorants, bald eagles, grackles, purple finches, teal, sandhill cranes and numerous geese?

A. John James Audubon.

———◆———

Q. How many state operated fish hatcheries are there in Tennessee?

A. Eight.

———◆———

Q. Who became the first state geologist in 1831 and was noted for writing a large volume of literature concerning the geological, paleontological, and mineralogical aspects of Tennessee?

A. Gerard Troost.

———◆———

Q. Water from what resort in Grainger County was shipped all over the nation?

A. Tate Springs.

———◆———

Q. By 1940, twenty-one hydroelectric plants of the Tennessee Valley Authority were delivering how many kilowatt hours of electricity?

A. 3.19 billion kilowatt hours per year.

Q. What was mined in many Tennessee caves during the War Between the States and processed for the production of gun powder?

A. Saltpeter.

———◆———

Q. Which physiographic area contains the most natural bridges?

A. Cumberland Plateau.

———◆———

Q. What two types of foxes are found in the state?

A. Red and gray.

———◆———

Q. Who was the Wilson County agriculturalist who developed a strain of corn that produced two ears of corn per stalk, compared to previous varieties that produced only one ear per stalk?

A. William Haskell Neal.

———◆———

Q. Animaland's Special Riders program in Williamson County provides horseback riding lessons for what group?

A. Handicapped children.

———◆———

Q. Who was the biochemist born in Columbia who developed the serum to prevent hog cholera?

A. Marion Dorset.

———◆———

Q. The Eastern Red Cedar is in reality what type of tree?

A. Juniper (*Juniperus virginiana L.*).

Q. An extract from the bark of what flowering tree was used by Indians and later by early settlers in Tennessee to treat fevers.

A. Dogwood.

◆

Q. In August of 1843, a prospector named Lemmons discovered what mineral in Polk County?

A. Red oxide of copper.

◆

Q. What county is known for its fossil findings of the Silurian period of the Paleozoic era of shell-forming sea animals, fish, reef-building corals and sponges?

A. Decatur County.

◆

Q. Which two mining communities in Anderson County led the state for several years in the late 1800s?

A. Coal Creek (now Lake City) and Briceville.

◆

Q. Who originated the Lookout Mountain Park in Chattanooga?

A. Adolph S. Ochs.

◆

Q. When was the Tennessee Ornithological Society organized?

A. 1915.

◆

Q. How many types of fungi have been collected in the Great Smoky Mountains National Park?

A. Approximately 2,000 kinds.

Q. What is the smallest mammal in Tennessee?

A. Short-tailed shrew.

———◆———

Q. At what hospital did the nation's first in vitro fertilization take place?

A. Vanderbilt Hospital, Nashville.

———◆———

Q. What is the largest variety of owl found in Tennessee?

A. Great horned.

———◆———

Q. Since state records have been kept, what winter season has had the greatest snow fall?

A. Winter, 1959–1960.

———◆———

Q. The Tennessee Scenic Parkway System has how many miles of roads?

A. Over 2,300.

———◆———

Q. How many varieties of hummingbirds are found in Tennessee?

A. One (ruby-throated).

———◆———

Q. The Moss Island State Waterfowl Refuge is situated in what West Tennessee county?

A. Dyer.

Q. What four hides were most often sought after by the early long hunters of Tennessee?

A. Deerskins, buffalo hides, beaver pelts and bear furs.

Q. The Lost Sea in Loudon County is an underground lake made up of how many acres?

A. Four and one-half acres.

Q. Where in Tennessee does the largest population of bald eagles winter?

A. Reelfoot Lake.

Q. When was the first electric light viewed in Nashville?

A. May 1, 1882, in the second story of the Capitol.

Q. The Tertiary (Eocene) clays of West Tennessee contain large amounts of what type of fossils?

A. Leaves.

Q. What schoolteacher was convicted of teaching evolution in a Tennessee public school?

A. John Scopes.

Q. What did the Cherokee Indians bring DeSoto in June of 1540 when his expedition camped near their village?

A. Twenty basket of mulberries.

◆

Q. What material was used to line the fireplaces of log cabins?

A. Clay.

◆

Q. What is the highest temperature ever recorded in Tennessee?

A. 113 degrees Fahrenheit (August 9, 1940, Perryville).

◆

Q. Couchville Lake, adjacent to Percy Priest Reservoir, was formed by water from the reservoir filling a depression by backing up through what type of natural formation?

A. A large sinkhole.

◆

Q. Why did the federal government establish the Tennessee Valley Authority?

A. To conserve and develop the resources of the Tennessee River Valley.

◆

Q. Where in Nashville can animals native to Tennessee be observed in a natural environment?

A. Grassmere Wildlife Park.

◆

Q. What was the name of a black-and-tan hound stolen out of Pickett County in November of 1852 that became the foundation sire of all Walker, Trigg and Goodman fox hounds?

A. Tennessee Lead.

Q. What item was John Ruch first to import from France into Tennessee, greatly improving the agricultural economy?

A. Crimson clover seed.

Q. Naturalist John Muir passed through Tennessee in what year on his famous 1,000 mile walk from Kentucky to Florida?

A. 1867.

Q. Where was the first ginko imported from Japan planted in Tennessee?

A. On the grounds of Ashwood Hall near Columbia.

Q. Near what community is black-veined marble to be found?

A. Rutledge in Grainger County.

Q. Who was the physician born in Greene County who was the first person to successfully graft skin from a dead body to a living one?

A. John Harvey Girdner.

Q. What are the two species of bats found in Tennessee?

A. Gray bat (*Myotis griescens*) and Indiana bat (*Myotis sodalis*).

Q. Who was called the "Father of Tennessee Archaeology" and authored *Antiquities of Tennessee*?

A. Gates P. Thurston.

Q. How many times does the Tennessee River cross the state?

A. Twice.

Q. Because of the heavy haze, what did the Cherokees call the mountains of East Tennessee?

A. The land of a thousand smokes.

Q. Southern States Limes Corporation plant produces high grade lime in which county?

A. Cumberland County.

Q. What is the state record for a largemouth bass?

A. 14 lb. 8 oz., Sugar Creek.

Q. What percentage of Tennessee land area is forested?

A. More than one half.

Q. The Tennessee Wildlife Resources Act was passed in what year?

A. 1974.

Q. Which large manufacturer in Middle Tennessee was the first to use robotics extensively?

A. Nissan, in Smyrna.

Q. Where was the state record bluegill caught?

A. Fall Creek Falls, weighing three pounds.

Q. For what reason was June 20, 1873, known in Nashville as "Black Friday"?

A. There were 72 cholera-related deaths on that date.

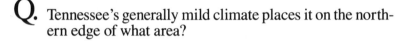

Q. How many miles of streams are there in this state?

A. 19,000 miles.

Q. Tennessee's generally mild climate places it on the northern edge of what area?

A. The Sun Belt.

Q. What are the official state rocks of Tennessee?

A. Limestone and agate.

Q. Where is the largest pecan tree in the world to be found?

A. Natchez Trace State Park.

Q. At which reservoir was the state record muskellunge (muskie) caught?

A. Norris Reservoir, weighing 42 pounds 8 ounces.